Navigating Tricky Conversations Skillfully

A "Connective Communication" primer for couples, coaches and communication enthusiasts

A Healthy Relationships production

By Yogi Ramadin

Copyright © 2015 Yogi Ramadin

All rights reserved. This book may not be reproduced in part or entirety, or transmitted in any form without written permission from the publisher, excepting common fair use standards; nor may any part of this book be reproduced, stored in a retrieval system or transmitted in any way or by electronic, mechanical, photocopying, recording, in person workshop or other means without written permission from the publisher.

The information contained in this book is for educational purposes. This information should not replace consultation with a qualified psychologist, therapist or coach. This book is designed to support and empower rational self responsibility. The author and publisher are in no way liable for any results the reader obtains through the use or misuse of this information.

ISBN-13: 978-0692378472
ISBN-10: 0692378472

I invite you to express what feels true for you in a way that enlivens your spirit with a sense of possibility.

~ Yogi Ramadin

Preface

Thank you for reading this book!

After years of study, field application and personal integration work, I find myself standing on the shoulders of giants and sharing with you just a glimpse of what I see from here. What follows is a synthesis of many contributions made by far too many people to mention. In a wide sweep, I will tell you that this text is informed by Humanistic Psychology, Yogic Philosophies, Compassionate Communication and more.

This book started out as an instruction booklet for a communication education and facilitation tool that I created, called the "Communication Journey Kit."

Once the Communication Journey Kit was created, I realized that it wasn't enough to simply tell people how to use the kit. What they really needed was strong background and understanding in human conversational tension dynamics and how to navigate them gracefully.

It is my intention to share this information with you so that you may empower yourself and your communities in creating more trust, deeper intimacy and greater compassion through understanding of self and others.

I am most excited about the power of Body Wisdom and its potential to unite our subconscious mind and our conscious mind. Please pay special attention to how Body Wisdom applies in your own life.

I am intending to expand this text, so if there are sections that are not clear or you would like to see expanded, please contact me using the information in the Next Steps chapter.

This book would not be possible without the support of my friends and ancestors. Thank you to so many people who put energy forward into humanity so that my life and this experience is even possible.

Thank you to my Mother who bore me into this world.

Thank you to my Father who provided for me and taught me about self-reliance.

Thank you to mother earth, who continues to support, feed and shelter me and so many others.

Thank you to Abraham Maslow, the Father of Humanistic Psychology for introducing the Hierarchy of Needs and the truth of interdependence.

Thank you to Nikola Tesla, who gifted more to humanity than can be fully comprehended. Thank you for liberating us with motorized equipment, harnessing the marvel of Alternating Current and uniting us with the power of communication over a distance.

Thank you to any and every person who has ever done yoga or any personal healing work or taken care of their own health and well being for any reason.

Thank you to scholars and poets alike who keep spirituality alive in their own daily works.

And thank you, to YOU, the reader, for taking the time to invest in your own life and your competency in skillful interpersonal relating. May this text be an asset to you and inspire many Connective Communications that flow into rewarding friendships.

Warmly,

Yogi Ramadin

Thank you also to my Editors and Contributors.

Julie Barr MA, LMFT
Alissa Blackman MA, LMFT
Reverend Taber Shadburne MA
Deborah Wiig Communications

Navigating Tricky Conversations Skillfully

i. **Introduction**
   i. Whom is this Book For?
   ii. How this Book is Organized
   iii. Introducing the Communication Journey Kit
   iv. Pitfalls
   v. Tips

Part 1: Guiding Principles
1. **Goals / Intentions**
   1.1. Key Intentions
   1.2. Stated Goals
   1.3. Unstated Goals
   1.1. Goals of Others
2. **Conversation Climate**
   2.1. Conversation Resources
   2.2. Contributing Conditions
   2.3. Conversation Emotional Climate
   2.4. Navigating Emotional Conversations
   2.5. What Conversation Mode Should I Use?
3. **Warmth And Collaboration**
   3.1. Appreciation
   3.2. Posture of Collaboration
   3.3. Allurement
   3.4. Safe-porting
   3.5. Crafting Conversation Invitations
4. **Conversation Pacing**
   4.1. Conversational Tension
   4.2. Effective Pacing and Shared Meaning
   4.3. Preventing and Repairing Blowout
5. **Body Feedback and Intuitive Wisdom**
   5.1. Cognitive Dissonance
   5.2. Somatic Resonance
   5.3. Transference
   5.4. Diffusion and Integration

Contents

6. Yogic Approaches
- 6.1. Yamas and Niyamas
- 6.2. 4 Yogic Keys for Interpersonal Relating
- 6.3. Cognitive Mindfulness and Liberating Language
- 6.4. Noticing Resistance to Joy

Part 2: Using the Communication Framework

7. Communication Framework
- 7.1. Roles
- 7.2. Goals and Intentions
- 7.3. Communication Modes
  1. Soft Modes
  2. Moderate Modes
  3. Assertive Modes
  4. Shadow Modes

8. The Communication Cycle
- 8.1. Consider Your Intention
- 8.2. Set Up the Cards if Available
- 8.3. Establish Conversation Roles
- 8.4. Establish Conversation Intentions
- 8.5. Invite Collaborator(s) to a Round
- 8.6. Using Moderation Cards and Tokens
- 8.7. End with an Appreciation Round

Part 3: Improving Your Conversational Competence

9. Additional Tips for Navigating Tricky Conversations
- 9.1. Should There Be a Conversation Facilitator?
- 9.2. Providing Support, One at a Time!
- 9.3. Hearing the Story, One at a Time!
- 9.4. Learn to Identify Communication Modes

10. Facilitating Tricky Conversations
- 10.1. The Myth of Understanding
- 10.2. Monitoring Conversational Resources
- 10.3. Navigating Climates
- 10.4. Conversation Pacing
- 10.5. Verbally Naming Modes In Use
- 10.6. Conversational Coherence

Navigating Tricky Conversations Skillfully

11. **Examples**
    - 11.1. Setting Intentions
    - 11.2. Create Conversation Invitations
    - 11.3. Verbally Name Modes In Use
    - 11.4. Reorient to the Conversation Intention
    - 11.5. Reorient to the requested Conversation Mode
    - 11.6. Closure with Appreciation
12. **Doing Your Own Self-Study**
    - 12.1. Collect all the Communication Modes
    - 12.2. Use All 4 Yogic Keys
    - 12.3. Observe Emotional Climates
13. **Next Steps**
    - 13.1. Complete the Self Study
    - 13.2. Watch Connective Communication Videos Online
    - 13.3. Join the Connective Communication Newsletter
    - 13.4. Order the Communication Journey Kit
    - 13.5. Give This Book As A Gift
    - 13.6. Request Facilitation
    - 13.7. Request Group Training
    - 13.8. Take the Personal Immersion Training
    - 13.9. Become a Connective Communication Coach
    - 13.10. Submit Feedback
14. **Bibliography**
15. **Index**

Contents

Navigating Tricky Conversations Skillfully

Introduction

Welcome to *"Navigating Tricky Conversations Skillfully,"* a "Connective Communication" primer for couples, coaches and conversation enthusiasts.

This book can be used alone or with the "Communication Journey Kit" to introduce helpful concepts in facilitating Connective Communication.

I have included pictures and descriptions of the Communication Journey Kit cards in this book. With understanding of the concepts in the cards and the materials within this handbook, you should be able to begin facilitating your own conversations more skillfully toward your own goals and the goals of others.

In this section, we will explore:

- Whom is this book for?
- Introducing the Communication Journey Kit
- Pitfalls
- Tips

Whom is this Book For?
- Conversation Enthusiasts
- Couples
- Families
- Office Workers
- Conversation Facilitators: Psychologists, Coaches, MFT's, Lawyers, Business Negotiators

While it is obvious that the approaches outlined herein can be useful for mitigating family and relationship conflicts, it's also worth keeping in mind that these approaches are also very helpful in the workplace and in sales.

For example, marketing researchers have found that people largely make purchases based on emotion and then rationalize their decision later with supporting data.

> "Emotion is the KEY to every decision we make, every thought we have... Human beings tend to take everything personally and respond with feeling." - Kevin Roberts [Russel & Lane 2002]

What this means is, if you are able to support people in feeling great about an idea, then they are likely to "buy" your idea or product. So whether you are striving to pitch that upcoming trip to your spouse or to customers of your travel agency, Safe-porting, checking-in, appreciating and creating Somatic Resonance can all play a big part in getting "buy-in" and group agreement.

Office environments that encourage virtuous communication approaches are likely to have greater team coherence leading to higher efficiency and less sick time.

How this Book is Organized
When considering sharing the "Communication Journey Kit," I realized that I wanted more than just support people in using the

kit. I wanted to support people in having profound satisfaction in relating. While it may be tempting for some readers to jump straight to the sections about the Communication Framework, I feel it's essential for conversationalists to approach relating with certain fundamental postures.

If conversationalists charge ahead without the fundamentals, then they risk the dangers of starting off on the wrong foot and possibly doing more harm than good.

Consequently, I have separated the book into three parts:

- Part 1: Guiding Principles
- Part 2: Using the Communication Framework
- Part 3: Improving Your Conversational Competence

Ideally, conversationalists will remain mindful of the guiding principles while they are using the framework. Since achieving mastery is a progression, I recommend revisiting Part 1 often and considering how each of the elements relates to your own life and consciousness. The guiding principles are as important, if not more important than the framework itself.

Introducing the Communication Journey Kit

This book you are reading now emerged from the creation of the Connective Communication Framework. The framework was originally created on 3x5 note-cards and then transformed into graphic cards with informative text. I then needed to create a user's manual for the card kit. I decided that simply describing the parts of the kit was not adequate. What I wanted to do was to help many people have satisfying conversations.

What has emerged now is this book, which contains snapshots of the Connective Communication cards and also rich discussion regarding many aspects of communication. The framework was designed as a concept and as such can be used in the field with or without the Communication Journey Kit. The kit just makes it easy to introduce others and to keep the conversation grounded by externalizing the process and breaking the conversation down into manageable parts.

What is the Communication Journey Kit?

This communication tool is designed to facilitate heart- and spirit-opening conversations, otherwise known as Connective Communication.

The Communication Journey Kit is a toolkit that introduces people to setting intentions, establishing conversational roles and using communication modes. During a conversation journey, participants can pick an Intention Card and Conversation Mode Card to explore a particular topic together. While in a Conversation Round, use Appreciation Tokens and Speaker Moderation Cards to influence the conversation pace. Appreciation Tokens also offer an additional means to stay connected and develop alliance without interrupting the speaker.

Individuals using the kit are introduced to modes and skillful strategies that they can use in all conversations. Once you have become familiar with the modes and establish a practice of requesting specific modes, you will be able to do this casually in conversation even without the kit.

Why use the Communication Journey Kit?

- To learn approaches in Connective Communication
- To facilitate conversations
- To educate others about Connective Communication

When to use the Communication Journey Kit

Individuals and groups can use the Communication Journey Kit in the moment, when they need immediate support in keeping a conversation on track.

Participants are likely to get the best results in Connective Communication if they study it ahead of time with others or on their own to learn more about communication and understand the Communication Modes.

Introduction 17

You may want to introduce others to Connective Communication. You could share the kit with others at a party, meeting or meal to educate them about communication and introduce them to styles of communication that you might be wanting to use with them.

Check the Conversation Climate

Is it a "good time to talk" to get a collaborative discussion? Checking in with yourself and other conversation participants regarding these factors can assist you in getting your goals met by using mindful timing to schedule your conversation.

- Do the conversation participants have sufficient energy and attention to engage the discussion now?
- Is there enough time to discuss the topics of interest?
- Will there be any interruptions?
- Are any of the participants emotionally volatile?

What to Expect When Using the Kit

- Conversations may move more slowly.
- The framework may feel rigid at first.
- Expect yourself and others to have better mastery in asking for the type of conversational engagement you would like.
- You will learn to identify the conversation climate and skillfully respond to destructive conversation tactics.

On the Communication Journey Kit cards, you will see that each card has pitfalls and tips.

Here are a few pitfalls and tips to get you started before we journey into more specific tips on each concept.

Pitfalls

Pitfalls are areas where you might fall into a trap, wasting time and energy, or have your goals sabotaged. Keep an eye out for pitfalls while on your Conversation Journey.

- Be wary of engaging in conversations when participants are lacking sufficient attention, energy or interest.

- Be wary of engaging when there is insufficient time to engage in the conversation in a relaxed manner.
- Be wary of engaging when You or Conversation Collaborators are feeling emotionally volatile.

Tips

Tips keep potential hazards in mind and help us get the best results possible with the resources at hand.

- Review all the Communication Modes ahead of time and take time to understand them.
- Learn to spot Shadow Modes like Attacking, Defensive and Venting when they occur unannounced or unsolicited.
- Question potential Conversation Collaborators to agree upon a good time to have the desired conversation.
- Before you start, check-in with all participants concerning the conversation climate and amount of time available for the discussion.

Part 1: Guiding Principles

Chapter 1

Goals and Intentions

Whether they know it or not, Conversation Initiators will want to accomplish something through their actions of communication. It may be to alleviate some stress, to solve a problem or to influence others.

It is worth mentioning that usually goals are a measurable, achievable outcome. Intentions may be considered as something we want to strive towards but may not be easily defined by some clear deadline or end point.

For instance, a desire to be nicer to another person is not something that you will know when it's completed (goal.) It's a posture and way of being that one embodies in an ongoing way.

In this chapter, we will explore:

- Key Intentions
- Overt Goals
- Implicit Goals
- Goals of Others

Key Intentions

Without Key Intentions, conversations are ungrounded without any fundamental direction. When one considers the idea of "Navigating Tricky Conversations Skillfully," your Key Intentions are your compass to help guide you in staying true to your course. If you overtly state your intention to have things get better between you and another person, then you have laid the foundation to more easily reorient the conversation toward the intention originally stated.

Often times unmentioned, Key Intentions can be the most important and powerful element in creating conversational coherence.

Here are some examples of Key Intentions:

- mutual respect
- more pleasurable relating
- greater ease in relating
- shared understanding

Mentioning these intentions overtly can greatly help to create more trust and rapport.

Stated Goals

Stated Goals and Intentions are the changes that we are enthusiastic about discussing. For example, "Let's figure out who gets to park in the driveway on Friday evenings."

Stating an overt goal before creating mutually beneficial intentions can sometimes inhibit the collaboration process. This is because putting an operational need before the value of another person can be rude or offensive. In Connective Communication, it is recommended that you state an intention to take care of the relationship and honor the other person before requesting to make a strategic decision.

Unstated Goals and Intentions

Individuals often have complex agendas and many needs being met by various life situations. Considering this, they may be selective when sharing their stated goals and intentions. Also, if they have a goal that things stay the way they are, they may not mention it overtly. However, some unstated goals may really serve your cause if you take the time to state them.

Some examples of potentially unstated goals / intentions:

- to remain in a harmonious relationship
- to have a relaxed / friendly conversation
- to understand more about another person and their needs
- to have a relationship get better and have more fun
- to feel less stress about <your topic>

The Goals of Others

The more you represent understanding the needs and goals of others, the more successful and satisfying your conversations will be. Taking the time to consider the goals of others will not only have you more informed, but may also have you feeling and acting more compassionate toward them.

Later in this book I explain the processes of crafting conversational invitations and also Safe-porting. These methods work best when you have some understanding of the needs of others. If you read this and you are stumped, wondering, "How could I possibly know what their goals are?" you might try asking them.

Asking people about their goals and intentions is a great way to get them to share more about themselves and to create more rapport. Also fully understanding the goals of others may have you better equipped to come up with creative problem solving so that your mutual goals are no longer conflicting.

26   Navigating Tricky Conversations Skillfully

Chapter 2

Conversation Climate

Before any conversation starts, there is often some pre-existing circumstance that the current conversation emerges from. That situation may be creating tension within an individual or between individuals. These personal and interpersonal tensions and other factors all affect the Conversational Climate.

In this chapter, we will explore:

- Conversation Resources
- Contributing Conditions
- Conversation Emotional Climate

Conversation Resources

If you want to end your conversation on a positive note, you will want to be tracking the Conversational Resources. If you see that these resources are depleted, then it may be time to add some appreciation, propose ending the talk, take a break or schedule another discussion.

Some Conversation Resources include:
- Time: Is there enough for the conversation?
- Privacy: Will there be any interruptions?
- Emotional Stability: Are participants combative?
- Attention / Cognitive Availability/ Interest: Can participants continue to focus on the topic at hand?

Contributing Conditions

What are the relevant conditions, either to the conversation or just related to whomever is in the current conversation? Did someone just get come home from working a long day? Did someone get fired or lose a loved one? Is there a long standing history of volatile conversations?

These questions and more are all part of what makes up the context in which we have the conversation. Making adjustments based on the current conditions can be very helpful in creating a collaborative environment and have participants feel considered and valued.

Conversation Emotional Climate

You may notice conversation participants experiencing being
- Relaxed
- Tense
- Highly Reactive

You may also observe yourself or other participants engaging in

Chapter 2: Conversation Climate

potentially destructive conversation approaches. In Connective Communication, potentially destructive approaches are generally referred to as "Shadow Modes."

Emotional volatility is likely to happen when the conversation is not well resourced. You can read more about Conversational Resources in the Facilitation section.

Watch for any Shadow Modes being used. If you see a Shadow Mode being used, you can name it and request more collaboration.

Here are some examples of Shadow Modes:

- Attacking
- Defensive
- Dismissive
- Venting
- Invalidation
- Deflection

Reference the first three Shadow Modes in the Communication Modes section for more information. This list is not exhaustive. You may be able to name three or four more Shadow Modes of your own!

In later sections of this book, you can learn skills to improve the climate of the conversation as you go along.

To get the best results possible in the conversation, communicators should be respectful of the current Conversational Climate, responsive to the needs of all participants, and prepared to work collaboratively.

Navigating Emotional Conversations

Before going into conversation, you will want to consider the Emotional Climate. In situations where someone feels Emotionally Reactive, they may be REALLY SURE that they want to discuss the issue "RIGHT NOW." However, right now may not be the best time and climate in order to effectively accomplish your goals.

You may also want to consider:

- Is there emotional charge about the topics for anyone involved in the conversation?
- Are there other related or unrelated stressors affecting the situation?
- When might be the best time to propose a conversation in order to get good results?

Treat emotional conversations like unpacking. Once you have unpacked it enough, then you can easily see things and put them in their place. It takes a certain amount of time and energy unpacking and "airing things out" before they can go back to "right order."

Consider your goals and choose your conversational approach mindfully.

What Communication Mode should I use?

High volatility conversations often work best at a snail's pace using Soft Modes, especially Attentive Listening and Echoing. During high volatility is when Shadow Modes are most likely to emerge. Watch for Invalidation, Defensive, Venting, and Attacking.

Once emotionally reactive individuals have expressed themselves sufficiently using Soft modes they may experience situational and Emotional Diffusion and be able to then move into Moderate Modes such as Interpretation and Empathy.

If the emotional volatility is low, you may be ready for something more assertive like Advice or Devil's Advocate.

Chapter 2: Conversation Climate

32 Navigating Tricky Conversations Skillfully

Chapter 3

Warmth and Collaboration

In Benjamin Franklin's 1744 'Poor Richard's Almanac' he cites,

> "**Tart words make no friends; a spoonful of honey will catch more flies than a gallon of vinegar.**" [Franklin 1744]

To be clear, Benjamin Franklin is not talking about trapping flies. What he's suggesting in reciting G. Torriano's Italian Proverb is that we have a better chance of getting what we want, when we approach it with sweetness rather than being caustic.

While it's easy to agree that being sweet can keep the conversation feeling good and more sustainable for all, it's not always clear what being sweet actually means. Consequently, we will explore different flavors of sweetness and techniques we can use to create more warmth and collaboration.

In this chapter, we will explore:

- Appreciation
- Posture of Collaboration
- Allurement
- Safe-porting
- Crafting Conversation Invitations

Appreciation

If you have ever wanted more satisfaction in your life and in your conversations, pay close attention to this section.

Life is full of experiences that either cost us emotional and attention energy or revitalize us. Leaving conversations and work feeling exhausted is quite common, so we all know the dynamics of how experiences cost us time, energy and attention.

What is not quite so commonly understood is how our energy gets replenished by anything other than sleep. Later in this book you will read about Somatic Resonance. When we experience Somatic Resonance, it puts energy back into our system for use. The more Somatic Resonance you have with life, the more energized and activated you will be.

One of the easiest ways to achieve Somatic Resonance is with appreciation. With appreciation, we are figuratively saying Yes to some experience life has been offering us. By taking the time to appreciate those gifts in life, we actually get to experience the gifts more. The acts of appreciating fill us with life. If you want more gratitude in your own life, take time to appreciate what you have.

Similarly, sharing appreciation with another person can be emotionally and energetically satisfying for them as well. By taking the time to share with someone that you like what they said, how they said it or that they took the time to be with you and share, you are investing in trust building. The more genuinely appreciative you can be, the more interested they will be in coming to conversations with you in person. The more appreciation there is, the more satisfying life will be for you and those around you.

You may even begin to practice what some call a "Gratitude Practice" or a "Gratitude Lifestyle". If we make a practice of being appreciative before, during and after our interactions, then our lives become full of gratifying moments and we continue moving from a deeply nourished and fulfilled place.

Chapter 3: Warmth and Collaboration

If you aren't currently practicing a Gratitude Lifestyle, you can start it on your own by beginning your day acknowledging the gifts of breath, freedom to move and the ability to make our own choices in the world. If you are living a privileged life, then you could also be thankful for food, water and shelter. Starting from this place orients us to the scale of other problems and empowers us to move in equanimity.

In conversation, you can begin bringing in more gratitude by starting conversations with:

> "Thank you for taking the time to talk with me, I really appreciate you making this discussion a priority and being in the conversation."

In the middle of a conversation, you could offer something like:

> "Wow, thank you for offering that bit of insight. I can really understand you and the situation much better. I also appreciate what you have been going through and I'm glad you mentioned it to me."

After a conversation, you might conclude with:

> "Thank you so much for taking the time to talk with me. I know some parts of the conversation were stressful and I really appreciate you for staying loving and respectful with me while we were discussing the issue. Thank you also for keeping it safe for us to talk about it."

Take some time practicing each day. Look for little things to appreciate on your own and also in conversation. Notice how acknowledging that which fuels you, fuels you even more. As you invest more attention on that which fuels you, the more "mileage" you get out of it.

Posture of Collaboration

If you were to imagine looking at yourself and another person in a tricky conversation, do you think it would look more like a dance or a duel?

If you experience yourself in a posture that feels defensive or edgy then you may realize that these are actually words of war.

The word "posture" can refer not only to the way we are physically standing but also the way we are cognitively positioning ourselves and relating with the world. Different states of being are aspects of our posture.

While it's true that we can create collaboration through threat of force, we can get more sustainable relationships and more loyalty by valuing others with mutual respect and sweetness. When we are edgy with others, it creates more distance and less interest to relate. When we use threat of force, it can be perceived as an act of violence, oppression and manipulation. This threat of force undermines mutual respect and will invite destructive dynamics.

We can achieve a posture of collaboration when we respect others as worthy contributors. Requesting their presence and input to create an interaction that is satisfying for all strengthens the collaborative relationship. Living up to those words that were shared can also be an important part of the collaborative dance and creating lasting trust.

Allurement

How we represent the situation with others can have a great impact on their level of interest and availability to relate with us. If we share something that seems interesting or potentially satisfying with someone, they may be curious and want to engage more. However if we present something that seems offensive, stressful or chaotic they may resist or avoid it.

In Benjamin Franklin's quote at the beginning of this chapter, Benjamin is directly talking about Allurement.

Chapter 3: Warmth and Collaboration

Consider these two different approaches to the same situation. The situation is that person A is having stress and wants to resolve it with person B.

Using the "vinegar" approach, person A might say,

> "We Need to Talk!"

Person B would then most likely interpret a high amount of stress in the conversation and maybe have some fears about being blamed or stress about being in a high volatility conversation.

Using the "honey" approach, person A might say,

> "I notice that I'm really stressed out and I really want to be more relaxed and nicer to you. Would you be up for having a friendly conversation with me and help me in having it get better with us?"

In this example person A disarms some defensiveness in person B by taking responsibility for the chaos that they are creating. Then person A also offers a seduction of being nicer to person B. Person A then follows it up with reassurance, a request and offering the allurement of the situation improving for both person A and person B.

The "honey" approach is much more likely to create a collaborative engagement between person A and person B in two ways. The first and most obvious way is that it sounds much better to person B. But the second and more important way is that it represents and reinforces a desire in person A to be respectful to person B. It also creates a situation where person A is then committed to being warm and respectful with person B. In this way, the sweet request has an effect on both the speaker and the listener.

Safe-porting
To "Port" is to carry from one place to another. To Safe-port means

to carry from here to there in a safe means. Specifically in conversation we mean not only without incident, but more importantly in a way that feels "safe" to conversation participants. In order to feel safe we must identify what it is that there is a fear of and also identify what measures are being taken in order to protect from loss. Each person is unique in their own fears of loss, but understanding those fears can help you to effectively Safe-port them in a conversation invitation.

One simple example would be if you want to have a conversation with someone who has fears about being late for an upcoming appointment. To Safe-port them, you could bring them from a place of resisting the conversation to a place of discussion it by saying something like:

> "I know you have to leave two hours from now and it's really important to be on time and in a happy (emotionally grounded) disposition for your appointment. I was wondering if we could have a five minute conversation, which I envision to be very relaxed and have us both feeling more friendliness in the end. Do you think you are up for more fun and more friendliness in 5 minutes or less?"

Crafting Conversation Invitations

Mindfully crafted conversation invitations can get the conversation off to a great start in so many ways. Primarily, we start out the conversation from a place of respecting the other person, respecting that person's time, respecting their contribution to the discussion and being curious about their contribution. Additionally we are starting the conversation off from a place of Yes. As we have discussed, bringing more Yes into the conversation activates Somatic Resonance and has participants feeling more well resourced and simultaneously more relaxed. Most importantly,

Chapter 3: Warmth and Collaboration

before one makes an invitation, there is a process of consideration... What are the other person's needs? What kind of conversation would they agree to come to?

Conversation invitations also give an opportunity to create agreement about what the conversation will focus on. If there is agreement to talk about the driveway parking in a friendly way, when the conversation digresses into other subjects or becomes unfriendly then either participant can then re-state the agreement to be in a friendly conversation about the driveway. In this way, the original invitation becomes an anchor point to re-orient the conversation to a mutually rewarding conversation.

In crafting your own conversation invitations, it will be up to you to interpret the situation and to create an invitation that is respectful and alluring to potential participants. By understanding them and effectively appealing to their interests you will be able to create situations that are rewarding for everyone. This will continue to create more trust and collaboration as a result.

"Guerrilla Warfare" Conversation Style

Not everyone has the time or emotional capacity to gracefully manage every conversation at every moment of the day. "Guerrilla Warfare" conversationalists don't care about that. Guerrilla Warfare Conversationalists may spring a conversation on you at any time. Maybe even after a long day at work or in the middle of the hallway when the phone is ringing.

Guerrilla Warfare Conversations may have the Attacker feeling slightly less pressure in the moment because they were able to "get it off their chest" (Venting), but generally this style degrades trust and may result in people "hiding out" or being generally less available over time.

Saving Face With Invitations for Scheduling

Because life has its own flow, individuals may be more prepared at some times than others. Being able to plan ahead for a conversation may help your Conversation Collaborators be better prepared for a conversation.

For example, if you ask unexpectedly for a data point that a co-worker "should know", then the person may look or feel bad for not remembering the information at the moment. However, if they know ahead of time that they are going to be talking with you about "The Jones Case" then they could bring the information with them or review it beforehand. This gives everyone a chance to do their best and be well resourced for the conversation.

Aside from being more prepared with technical information, everyone in the conversation can also have a better chance of making sure they are well rested or have recently eaten or taken care of any other potential distractions that might get in the way of the conversation.

Chapter 3: Warmth and Collaboration

42   Navigating Tricky Conversations Skillfully

Chapter 4

Conversation Pacing

There are several ways to consider the conversation pace.

Conversations with high volatility or clear disagreement can have conversation participants feeling exhausted and disinterested quite quickly.

Meanwhile a conversation rich in resonant back and forth sharing and appreciation may go on for quite some time and leave participants feeling joyful and refreshed.

In an earlier segment of this book, I mentioned that emotional conversations are like unpacking. You need to have the space to unpack it and the time to air it out. You will also want to make sure that the conversation is well resourced.

In its more acute considerations, the pace may also refer to the back and forth of speaker and responder.

In this chapter, we will explore:

- Conversational Tension
- Effective Pacing and Shared Meaning
- Preventing and Repairing Blowout

Conversational Tension

Whether the conversation has emotional volatility or not, there is still most certainly a conversational tension. This tension can be in the form of anger or anxiety, but also can be in the form of creative tension. The pace of the conversation can also refer to how quickly or assertively one person transfers the conversational tension to the Conversation Collaborator.

If the Conversation Initiator has a lot of emotion associated with the topic and has recently put a significant amount of time and energy into the subject of interest, they may say quite a lot all at once in a very passionate way. This would be considered a fast paced conversation. If the responder is not ready for the fast pace, the conversation may end up being over before it even starts.

I discuss Conversational Tension further in the Body Wisdom chapter.

Effective Pacing and Shared Meaning

In Connective Communication, we have discussions in manageable segments of listening and responding.

This interplay of listening and response creates an affirmation of shared meaning.

If the pace of one communication participant is faster than another, then it becomes challenging or impossible to achieve shared meaning.

It may also be helpful to achieve a sense of balance of talking time between listener and responder. If one person dominates the talking time then it may be challenging to achieve affirmation of shared meaning.

It is also essential to understand the importance of Appreciation. Adding appreciation to a conversation can help to ease the stress of participants and enhance the satisfaction of all conversation participants.

Preventing and Repairing Blowout

Blowout is when a conversation ends abruptly, often with a sense of loss of collaboration, frustration or anger. This can easily occur when conversation participants are insensitive to pacing and using Shadow Modes.

- Use bite size pieces for all Communication Modes. Keep conversations simple to avoid blowout and exhaustion

- If you experience overload and waning attention ask for continuation of the conversation at a later time

- Good pacing creates an environment where there is more availability from each participant to come back to the conversation again soon.

- Start with short, collaborative communication cycles to create a good rapport between conversation participants to strengthen the relationship, and build cohesion.

- Verbally or physically express your appreciation whenever you are appreciating how a collaborator is showing up in the conversation or want to create more conversation resources
    - beginning: thanks for being here
    - middle: after a vulnerable reveal or acknowledgment
    - end: in thanks for the time shared on the topic

- Take responsibility: acknowledge your own stress and request a break or to discuss it more at another time

- Say Thank You! ESPECIALLY when it's hard. The easy road in the moment may be to walk away mad. The way the conversation ends is what people remember most. If you can be thankful for what was shared, even when it's hard, then you are well on your way to mastering Navigating Tricky Conversations Skillfully.

46   Navigating Tricky Conversations Skillfully

Chapter 5

Body Feedback and Intuitive Wisdom

In addition to speakers listening to each other, speakers and listeners both may want to consider listening to their own body as a somatic feedback device. By monitoring your body response, you can see if you are having a reaction to conversation. It can be quite powerful for a listener to check in with their body responses as another channel of communication.

However, this is a sophisticated level of awareness and may not be possible or necessary for some conversations.

In this chapter, we will explore:

- Cognitive and Somatic Tensions
- Cognitive Dissonance
- Somatic Resonance
- Transference
- Diffusion and Integration
- Why Choose Conflict?

Cognitive and Somatic Tensions

Whether tension is in our body or in our mind, it will certainly influence our behaviors. Furthermore, it is worth noting that Cognitive Tensions can evolve into Physical Tensions. Reciprocally, Physical Tensions can erode one's cognitive presence. Consequently it is wise to have approaches in both reducing Physical and Cognitive Tensions.

Continuing to focus on anxiety- or anger-producing thoughts creates more anxiety and anger. This increases both the Cognitive and Somatic Tensions. For example if someone continues to focus on an angering thought, their somatic tension is the elevated heart rate and the cognitive tension is the unexpressed thought projections that the thinker is waiting to express. The more thoughts they have that they want to express, the more cognitive and somatic tension build up.

Anger is only one example of emotion. These same dynamics apply to both destructive or creative tensions. It is also worth pointing out that tension in and of itself is not a bad thing. What I suggest striving for is graceful expression of these tensions that embody evolutionary progress.

A common contributor to emotional and cognitive tension is Cognitive Dissonance. In the upcoming segments I will discuss Cognitive Dissonance and its inverse, Somatic Resonance. I will also detail processes of Diffusion and Integration.

Cognitive Dissonance

Festinger states that:

> "Cognitive Dissonance is the feeling of discomfort when simultaneously holding two or more conflicting cognitions: ideas, beliefs, values or emotional reactions. In a state of dissonance, people may sometimes feel "disequilibrium":

Chapter 5: Body Feedback and Intuitive Wisdom

frustration, hunger, dread, guilt, anger, embarrassment, anxiety, etc." [Festinger 1957]

"How to Reduce Cognitive Dissonance
Kendra Cherry offers three key strategies to reduce or minimize Cognitive Dissonance: [Cherry n.d.]

- Focus on more supportive beliefs that outweigh the dissonant belief or behavior.
- Reduce the importance of the conflicting belief.
- Change the conflicting belief so that it is consistent with other beliefs or behaviors."

Why is Cognitive Dissonance Important?
Cognitive Dissonance tells us when we are in conflict with ourselves and our own accepted ideas. If we can tune in to recognizing Cognitive Dissonance in our body as an alarm bell to let us know that we may need to adjust course, then Cognitive Dissonance can be a means of navigating out of retaliatory or combative thought patterns.

While I offer many intellectual ideas in this book, I think this skill of identifying and taking responsibility for one's own Cognitive Dissonance is likely to be the most helpful in reducing self sabotaging behaviors and destructive conversations.

Somatic Resonance

The term Somatic Resonance is not yet popularized in the Psycho-Somatic communities, however I would like to popularize it here.

Just as Cognitive Dissonance can give us real time bodily feedback that something is not quite right, Somatic Resonance lets us know when we are on the right track or experiencing what we consider to be the "Truth" in the moment.

Individuals experiencing Somatic Resonance may report feeling more relaxed yet energized. Individuals may also report a softening of ego and a sense of deeper connection, compassion and understanding.

To experience Somatic Resonance, you can state something that you know to be 100% true and watch for any response in your body. Notice how your body relaxes at hearing "the Truth".

Why is Somatic Resonance Important?
Marketing research reveals that a higher percentage of consumers buy more frequently based on emotions rather than based on logic. What this means is that most of society is taking actions based on a response to how they are feeling. [Russel & Lane 2002]

The more you can get an individual saying "yes", the more relaxed and enlivened they will be and the more progress you can make in a conversation. This is the cumulative effect of Somatic Resonance. If you come to a conversation and share what feels True, then individuals will leave the conversation feeling more relaxed and energized than before. This sort of energizing activity can be powerful for building trust and connection over time.

How to Increase Somatic Resonance
A conversation participant can influence the amount of Somatic Resonance experienced by themselves and by others by choosing words wisely in a way that embodies or solicits more of the Truth or a statement of Yes.

For example, asking an individual what their name is, you would not likely get much Somatic Resonance. However, if you adjust your question and you already know the person's name, you could ask them, "Is your name Joe?" Joe would then say "Yes." This would result in a Somatic Resonance in Joe. Joe might experience having been asked a really simple question and rest into some ease in guessing that it's going to be an easy conversation. Joe might also feel more at rest and seen by you because you care enough to know his name.

Similarly, the questioning person (you) would also experience

Chapter 5: Body Feedback and Intuitive Wisdom

Somatic Resonance in having gotten through asking a question and getting a "yes." This creates an experience of Joe cooperating and creates a greater sense of relaxed forward momentum in the conversation.

If you don't have the information you need in order to get questions that result in a yes, you can ask open-ended questions and then reflect back what the speaker said in a way that entices them to answer yes.

Another usage of Somatic Resonance is to take a statement that has us feeling the effects of Cognitive Dissonance and rephrase the statement in several different ways. In this exercise one would watch for the difference in feeling response and interpret one's own body wisdom accordingly. One could also then use this emotional intelligence to be more "at choice" in how to approach a conversation. Reference the Liberating Language example on page 69 for more information.

There are more advanced levels of Somatic Resonance beyond what I have described here. It is worthy of an entire book on its own.

Exercise:

Step 1:

Spend five minutes talking with someone about something that angers or frustrates you. Write down what you notice about your heart rate, breath rate, tension and body temperature. Then ask your discussion partner if they noticed anything about your facial expressions, mannerisms and presence and note those also.

Sample: "My heart rate is elevated, jaw feels tense. I notice I'm not really breathing fully and my face is hot. I also feel like my guts are twisted up in knots. My exercise partner reported that I raised my voice, made a 'scrunchy eyebrow face' and used fast moving, grandiose hand gestures."

Then spend five minutes talking about something that brings you joy. Write down some notes about how your body feels at the end. Notice your body response and log how it's different than five minutes before.

Sample: "I feel relaxed, happy and energized. My heart and chest feels expansive and warm. My exercise partner reported that I smiled a lot, seemed very relaxed, yet energized. She also noted that I had my hand on my chest and was nodding my head in 'yes' while I was sharing my ideas."

In completing these activities you will attune to your own body wisdom and be able to recognize this body intelligence more while you are in conversation. You will see that talking about your anger using Terminal Language mostly leaves you feeling angry. You will also see that focusing your attention on the gifts of life have you feeling more fulfilled, relaxed and happy. These are direct examples of Cognitive Dissonance and Somatic Resonance.

Transference

There are several accepted definitions for Transference. For the sake of this discussion, we will define Transference as storing an emotional charge from a past experience within our body and then acting in response to the current moment and a past moment simultaneously. Transference creates an opportunity to vent this stored stress in our system. Unfortunately, it is often at the expense of a pseudo "innocent bystander".

For example, if a parent gets up at 6am to get ready for work after having been up all night, then gets delayed going to work by a sick child, and then gets delayed by a truck parked in front of the driveway, and waits for six red lights before arriving at work, there ends up being a huge stored up emotional charge around the idea of delays. Then when the person goes into the workplace and relates with a co-worker who is moving slowly and asks the parent to wait while they send a text message on their phone, the parent then gets irate and vents all of the built up frustration to the co-worker. In effect the emotional tension has been transferred to the co-worker, even though it did not start there.

How is Transference Useful?

Transference can be useful in showing us how we or other people could be loved and taken care of more.

Also, identifying what the foundational trigger is can be really helpful in getting the attention off the person who has become the object of the transference.

For example, a person might yell at a co-worker and then realize her outburst was uncalled for. She might reveal something like, "Oh I'm really sorry I yelled at you like that, I just can't handle being delayed any more today!"

Identifying Transference can aid you in DE-escalating a combative situation into a compassionate one.

If the person does not reveal their transference, a curious individual could inquire, "Wow it seems like you are really affected by this. Is there something more going on about this that I don't know about?" Be careful not to shame, blame or wrong the person about their level of reaction as to not elicit a defensive response.

Diffusion and Cognitive Integration

If we know we want to end a conversation feeling connected and relaxed, then there is an implied notion that interpersonal or intrapersonal tension may be in the way of our desired outcome.

Therefore a skillful conversation navigator will look for tensions within themselves and others and help to alleviate them, whether they are personal or interpersonal tensions.

Two polar opposites in tension relief are diffusion and integration. These polar opposites can often be used in tandem for deep resolution.

Diffusion

To understand diffusion we must consider the idea that "where attention goes, energy flows."

Let's say that you have a roommate who has done some chore for your house without fail for years. Now let's say that they neglect that chore for some reason at a really inconvenient time for you. Then, you spend the next five days brooding over how much of an inconvenience it was for you and how inconsiderate it was of them.

By spending more time with your attention on the incident in validating your case for being angry with them, you can actually build up more charge than the situation warrants. For example if it was a five minute mix-up, but then you spend five days getting angry about it, you have effectively escalated the issue and created additional charge on the situation.

An effective means of Diffusion is then to put the stressor into context. For example, spending some time appreciating and mentioning the span of years when the chore was done so well without question. If the amount of appreciation is increased, then one's focus and attention is on experiencing appreciation, thereby allowing anxiety to diffuse.

A more popular, yet slightly more risky diffusion strategy is Venting. If a person has been suppressing their own information and becoming angry about it, then they may develop a dire need to express this rising frustration. At first the statement or concern may be only 10 percent true, but if the truth is ignored for too long and unaddressed, then its perceived importance or perceived truth can increase. For example if a person is angry and suppresses it for months and then experiences other compounding stress, then they may convince themselves that the 10 percent truth is really 100 percent truth. In this case the person may not be able to DE-escalate their interpretation until after they have emphatically expressed their disdain through Venting. "You always..."

In another example, a person may be frustrated with living in a

Chapter 5: Body Feedback and Intuitive Wisdom

small town. Out of agitation they may say something like:

> "I hate this town! There is nothing to do here and it's so boring! All of the people here are jerks and there are no jobs!"

While it may be true that this person longs for something more inspiring or suitable to their own desires, it's likely not true that there are actually no jobs or that all the people are jerks. These are exaggerations as a result of compounded stress. After venting this statement, the person may follow up with:

> "OK, well, maybe not ALL the people are jerks and I guess there are a few jobs here that I don't really want. I guess I'm really just longing for more cultural diversity, evening community activities and something more globally connected than what I've been experiencing here."

Venting is a dangerous strategy because if someone does not use mindful speech, then they could just be compounding the problem by telling themselves aggravating stories. This danger can be reduced if the person doing the Venting is willing to use the venting as an opportunity to experience how it feels in their body to say each of the statements. They could even try saying the same statements repeatedly and watch for changes in their own somatic state while they are saying it.

Two much less dangerous approaches in diffusion are somatic reflection and focused breathing techniques.

In Somatic Reflection we simply state the response we notice in the body.

> "When I heard you say that, I noticed my jaw clenched and I stopped breathing. As I think about it now I can feel my heart start racing and my guts

56   Navigating Tricky Conversations Skillfully

feel all knotted up."

By using Somatic Reflection in this way, we stay out of the story of who is to blame or some other arguable point. Individuals can get out of inflammatory story making and just acknowledge the moment in their own body. Once this witnessing is done, often the body sensations will change and greater clarity emerges.

A slightly more complex method of diffusion is to use the preceding somatic awareness strategies in concert with mindful breath and an intention to be in a more relaxed, well-resourced place. Consider the lyrics of this powerful song titled Gold:

> "When the words are like bullets
> and they break through your skin,
> and there's no way to get them all out:
>
> When it feels like a rush
> seeping into your soul,
>
> Stay gold
>
> Stay gold
>
> Stay gold"
>
> [Yuna 2013]

In the lyrics of this song, Yuna is demonstrating a healthy approach of attention. I have previously cited that where attention goes, energy flows. There is Grace in these lyrics in that, she does not recommend not being affected by the problem. She does not recommend shooting back. She recommends putting your attention on embodying the healing vibration of loving eminence, repeatedly. The attention and intention is to embody love. This invokes both the inner experience of love and the outer expression

Chapter 5: Body Feedback and Intuitive Wisdom

of love.

If you could imagine that in your deepest places within your spirit, there is a deep well of golden healing light. The limitless power of the universe is always there for you to draw upon and bring light energy into your being. By setting one's intention to allow the love light energy of the universe into our essence, one is releasing attachment to the anxiety-provoking thoughts and effectively welcoming gold.

As that person continues to allow the gold energy to be expressed through them, they then share the loving gold energy with others. This can be expressed as being more grounded, relaxed and compassionate in conversation. This will also be expressed as a lower heart rate, a relaxed demeanor, and greater sense of alertness.

As a final stress reduction technique, it's worth mentioning Yogic Pranayama. Prana is life force energy and Pranayama exercises are often done in combination with focused breathing methods. There are many types of breathing methods. Some methods are for relaxation, some are for invigoration, and some are for harmonizing with other people.

What is most helpful to know on a basic level is that full or "complete" breathing begins with a complete exhalation followed by breathing progressively in to the lowest part of the belly by expanding the abdomen then breathing in to the mid-chest followed by expanding the upper ribs and breathing into the upper lung cavity. Once this complete breath in is completed, then begin the exhale from the tops of the lungs, down the chest and then fully collapsing the belly. When practicing this in rhythmical progression one may begin to see or sense a wheel-churning-type motion that builds the breath and Prana.

While doing this activity you can adjust its affects by changing the length of the in-breath and out-breath. Focusing on a slow rhythm with a longer out-breath will create a calming effect. A fast rhythm will create a more energizing effect.

Calming full breath techniques can be used before, during, and after tricky conversations.

To get greater Conversational Coherence and empathic attunement, you may try matching your breath at the same rate as other participants in the conversation. This practice embodies deep listening and your intention to be in tune with them. The action of listening paired with your intention to harmonize creates powerful physical, emotional, and energetic results.

Please keep in mind that the study of Pranayama is wide and deep. What I have shared here is a tiny introduction to the subject.

Cognitive Integration

In modern culture, we don't fully realize the extent to which we each program our own minds with the conscious / unconscious meanings and emotional posture we attach to every idea.

People will subconsciously choose a particular emotional posture based on what they believe will serve them best. All new and existing ideas pass through mental filters where we attach meaning. How do I feel about this? How do I want to relate to this? What is my posture or stance? What are my judgments about this idea?

This process then feeds into the way we relate with the world and how we make meaning with others. The way we think affects the way we speak. The way we speak affects our relationships and outcomes with others. So, at the heart of it, the way we are making meaning and interpreting our reality has a huge impact on the life we are living and what is to come of it in the future.

Thankfully in the journey of making meaning, we have our own inner guidance system. Cognitive Dissonance raises the flag to us that we have conflicting ideas that may require some type of re-framing or new information in order to achieve greater inner harmony.

Chapter 5: Body Feedback and Intuitive Wisdom

When we recognize Cognitive Dissonance we have an opportunity to adjust our meanings or create new meaning and surrender old ideas. This is the integration process. Integration is the process of our own evolution in our journey to greater wholeness. As we travel in the world and gain greater exposure and understanding, we find that previous belief systems may become outdated.

We all have the power to program our own minds in a way that is in concert with our own authenticity and the present moment. Creating meaning in this way is the essence of Liberating Language. It is a process of creating meaning in our own minds in a way that creates emotional and spiritual liberation. You can learn more about Liberating Language in the next chapter.

Why Choose Anger / Conflict?

"Can you believe what they did to me!? I'm totally right to be angry!"

People continue to be in conflict with themselves and others as long as they want to be. This may seem somewhat counter-intuitive and you may be thinking, "Why would someone choose to be in conflict?"

On a very simplistic level, we can consider whether we are welcoming, defended or open about any idea. When ideas don't serve us, or move against our intentions, we become defended about them. That is, we hold them at a distance. We hold those ideas as outside of ourselves and not serving us.

Individuals are always right to be in whatever emotional state they experience or choose to create for themselves.

The first step in getting out of conflict is acknowledging that the other person is totally right and maybe even justified in being angry or sad or whatever emotion they may be feeling. Without changing anything, they are totally right. Presenting this disarms the defensive position on their current emotional state.

If the person is seen as right in having the emotion, they often are

Navigating Tricky Conversations Skillfully

able to be witnessed in that emotion long enough to reach integration, compassion, and present moment wholeness.

If simply witnessing them and reflecting is not satisfactory, you may want to ask them directly whether or not they would like to work it out at this time. You may find that they may not be ready for collaboration or there is currently work that needs to be done in order for a posture of collaboration to be attained.

By using the strategies outlined in the Somatic Resonance section, you can get to deeper integration by supporting the person to be heard more fully. Once both the Conversation Initiator and the Conversation Collaborator have sufficiently engaged the topic matter with richness ending in Somatic Resonance, new stories, postures, and realities can begin to emerge from a place of deeper understanding and liberated personal choice.

This may require deeper work of transforming attachment, cleaning up self-talk with right mindfulness and cleaning up lifestyle habits of self-sabotage.

Chapter 5: Body Feedback and Intuitive Wisdom

62 Navigating Tricky Conversations Skillfully

Chapter 6

Yogic Approaches

As a result of thousands of years of research, tradition and development, the fundamental philosophies of Yoga have been cultivated by, tested and improved on by countless sages, devotees and scholars who committed lifetimes to creating practices that serve humanity.

The fundamental basis for any yoga practice, before any postures or poses or activity, is Mindfulness. Without Mindfulness, no yoga is there. Yogic Mindfulness is composed of what Westerners might consider as Do's and Don'ts for creating a Graceful life.

In this chapter we will explore:

- Yamas and Niyamas
- 4 Yogic Keys for Interpersonal Relating
- Liberating Language
- Noticing Resistance to Joy

Yogic Yamas and Niyamas: Restraints and Observances for Graceful Conversation

We will list the Yamas and Niyamas and a few ways in which they could apply to conversation approaches.

Please keep in mind that what I have mentioned here about Yamas and Niyamas is a gross simplification and that many volumes have been written on Yamas and Niyamas. They are listed here so that people who are already familiar with those concepts can see how Connective Communication correlates with Yogic principles.

Yamas

The five Yamas, otherwise known as "Restraints" could be considered the Don't Do's of Yogic living:

- **Ahimsa**: non-harming
    - ~ Refrain from violent language and Shadow Modes
    - ~ Refrain from repressing or minimizing other beings
- **Satya**: truthfulness / authenticity
    - ~ Don't tell lies or mislead others by omission etc.
- **Asteya**: non-stealing
    - ~ Don't ask for someone's time in advice when you really just want to vent
    - ~ Refrain from "Guerrilla Warfare" Conversations
- **Bramacharya**: moderation
    - ~ Approach the conversation in manageable portions
    - ~ Refrain from overly indulging in depreciating attentions
- **Aparigraha**: non-attachment
    - ~ Come to the conversation with curiosity about how it will work out and to learn the perspective of others

Niyamas

The five Niyamas, otherwise known as "Observances," could be considered the Do's of Yogic living.

- **Saucha**: purity
    - ~ Use virtuous conversational approaches
    - ~ Cite specific examples rather than generalizing
    - ~ Create healthy thinking and speaking habits
- **Santosha**: contentment
    - ~ Treat someone as a human being worthy of respect, even if you don't agree with their decisions or opinions. Each person has their place and their path.
- **Tapas**: discipline
    - ~ Use right timing when engaging with others
    - ~ Create mindful conversation intentions
    - ~ Be considerate of the emotional climate and the needs of others
    - ~ Restrain irrational emotional urgency
    - ~ Increase your stamina for uncomfortable conversations
- **Svadhyaya**: self-study
    - ~ Understanding and owning your own emotional reactions and logical inner workings
- **Isvara Pranidhana**: surrender / devotion
    - ~ Control is an illusion,
    we each resent or enjoy
    opportunities
    to contribute
    our influence

If you are inspired to explore Yamas and Niyamas more fully, please know that they can be applied widely in your life and serve to aid us in embodying greater Grace. Applying these to your life can be an ever-deepening, lifelong mindfulness practice.

4 Yogic Keys for Interpersonal Relating

In Yoga Sutra 1.33, Patanjali introduces "The Four Locks & Four Keys." The keys are broken down into two keys for emotional states and two keys for behavior types. [Satchidananda 2008]

The two keys for emotional states are:
- Friendliness for happy people
- Compassion for the suffering

For happy people, you may use a moderate or assertive mode with them, such as Check-in or Inspiration.

For someone who is suffering, you would want to use Soft Modes, such as Attentive Listening or Echoing. Do not give advice to people who are suffering. They are usually under-resourced and not ready to take on the responsibility of doing something new or different. Even if they ask for advice, in most cases emotionally reactive people really just want Attentive Listening, Echoing, Empathy or possibly Interpretation.

The two keys for behavior types are:
- Delight in the virtuous behavior
- Disregard (or indifference, or equanimity or detachment) toward the non-virtuous behavior

Similarly to happy people, for virtuous behavior, you may use a moderate or assertive mode with them like Check-in or Inspiration.

What does Patanjali mean when he advises us to use disregard toward Non-Virtuous Behavior?

Patanjali means, don't cling to Shadow Modes or engage them. Name Shadow Modes and bring the conversation back to virtuous modes (Soft, Moderate and Assertive Modes). If you engage in advising about desisting non-virtuous behavior, you actually encourage the negativity by resisting it. If you can let go of the non-virtuous behavior and re-orient focus to virtuous intentions, you will get further with your Conversational Resources.

Cognitive Mindfulness and Liberating Language

Our life now and in the future is a direct result of what we think and how we speak in the present. Therefore it is a worthy endeavor to use discernment about how we choose to make meaning with our words and even our thoughts in everyday life.

Some ways of speaking and making meaning in the world serve to liberate us in a physical and even a spiritual way. When we speak the Truth, sensations can often be felt as though a weight has been lifted or as a greater sense of relaxed aliveness.

In fostering more of this relaxed aliveness or "Somatic Resonance," some specific observances and restraints can be most helpful.

"Where attention goes energy flows"

If Joe spends 30 minutes thinking about what a bad person Suzie is because of what she did to him, then what Joe gets is 30 minutes of added frustrated from dealing with a bad person. If Joe spends 30 minutes considering all the ways that Suzie has helped and supported him in the past then he builds appreciation, which becomes a Conversational Resource.

Terminal Language

Terminal Language is the use of words that limit possibility. Terminal Language is often an exaggeration of the actual truth in order to make an inflammatory attack. Terminal Language is most easily spotted with the use of Always and Never.

"You Always Park in my Parking Spot!"

or

"I Never Get to Park in the Driveway!"

Navigating Tricky Conversations Skillfully

Negative Assertions

Negative Assertions project energy toward the undesired outcome. Negative Assertions are often expressed with an inquisitive tone as if to invite the listener to reassure the speaker to the contrary. By their very nature, Negative Assertions bring conflict.

For example, two people are in a car approaching a location and the driver parks on the street outside the house. The passenger then says inquisitively,

> "You're not going to park in the driveway?"

This negative assertion expresses disapproval of parking on the street and pressures the driver to either park in the driveway or explain why they did not. This could elicit a defensive posture from the driver as they experience the passenger's disapproval. It would be much more harmonious for the passenger to request,

> "Would you be willing to park in the driveway?"

Liberating Language

Liberating Language is speaking about the world in a way that empowers possibility by putting attention into actions in a way that has desired outcomes being well-resourced.

Liberating Language is inspired by the application of Yogic Yamas and Niyamas to the process of making meaning and creating perceived reality.

One aspect of Liberating Language is replacing terminal language with specific information:

> "I noticed that last Tuesday and Wednesday your car was parked in my parking spot"

Another aspect of Liberating Language is speaking in a way that creates more Somatic Resonance.

Instead of saying something like:

> "Yeah, this is my bad knee, it always hurts and I'm never going to walk again."

Someone using Liberating Language might say something like:

> "I'm learning to listen to my body and take better care of myself."

or

> "I'm taking extra time to give my leg lots of love and support."

or

> "I'm learning to enjoy moving at a slower pace."

Some of these phrases may seem like flowery pontification that has no roots in the truth. What is important here for using these techniques is to listen to your own words, notice how your body responds and see what feels true and satisfying to say.

You might consider several different statements and compare how each statement may feel differently in your body when you say it. You might even find that in saying a phrase several times, your body may feel slightly different each time. For example if we believe it more each time, we can get more in alignment with our Yes and feel more alive. However if we feel more annoyed each time, it may feel less and less true each time the phrase is spoken.

Liberating Language puts the aliveness of life into our words and every-day moments.

Say only what feels true for you and what enlivens / liberates your own spirit with a sense of possibility.

Noticing Resistance to Joy

Sometimes conflict happens when one person is in a good mood and another person is not in a good mood. This can be either temporary or more of an ongoing strategy for manipulation.

In some cases individuals may be acutely triggered by a situation and momentarily feel frustrated, sad or irritable. During that time, they are still in the act of experiencing how they are feeling and may be self-righteous, "This is why I feel this way!"

In more chronic situations, where someone is continuously disappointed, sad, frustrated, etc, it may be worth considering whether the person is an "Energy Vampire" and using negative tension as a way to recruit the attention and energy of others to be focused on them. "Misery loves company..." and your attention.

Before engaging with a person who seems to be coming from an emotionally low or reactive place, make an assessment of what is needed. Often people coming from a low place will say that they want advice or "help" and usually what they mean is they want to talk it out for themselves and have someone else listen or act as a sounding board.

Being seen and heard can make a huge difference for some people in some situations. As previously mentioned, someone who is emotionally charged may feel even more benefit by repeating themselves several times. In these times, just being able to be present and listen to these expressions can be a real gift to the person who needs to express themselves. Once they have the opportunity to express, they may have less resistance to joy.

Be mindful to regulate your own time, energy and availability.

It's also worth asking yourself, do I have any resistance to joy? Is there anywhere in my body that I could feel more joyful right now or allow myself to feel more alive? If the answer is yes, notice your own resistance to joy and allow that resistance to dissipate if you want to. This can even be practiced as a 5- or 10-minute meditation.

Chapter 6: Yogic Approaches

72 Navigating Tricky Conversations Skillfully

Part 2: Using the Communication Framework

Chapter 7

Communication Framework

The Connective Communication Framework was designed to help individuals consider any conversation, figure out the underlying intention, figure out who the initiator of the conversation is and how to relate with the conversation in a way that is most likely to satisfy the goals of all involved.

In the upcoming sections we will explore:

- Conversation Roles
- Conversation Intentions
- Communication Modes

Using these concepts you can more effectively navigate conversation toward a more grounded and connected outcome. Read ahead to explore each of the framework sections.

Conversation Roles
What is the importance of Roles?

By having specific Conversation Roles, participants are able to make focused progress on a specific topic with reduced risk of getting DE-railed from the Conversation Intention. Participants are able to engage the subject matter more deeply with a higher chance of satisfaction and interpersonal connection. Also, agreeing to and honoring the roles can be seen as an overt demonstration of intention to collaborate. This can be especially important in tense conversations.

What are the Conversation Roles?

- Conversation Initiator
- Conversation Collaborator
- Conversation Facilitator

The Conversation Initiator often has an idea of the Conversation Intention and what sort of mode they might like Conversation Collaborators to engage with. The Conversation Initiator is the best person to guess what the climate is, what pacing might work and what points need to be addressed.

Facilitators work to maintain integrity of the conversation. You can learn more about Conversation Facilitators in Chapter 10.

It is worth mentioning that the other remaining role is "Conversation Collaborator." By recognizing someone as a Conversation Collaborator, we are acknowledging that they are someone we value and respect and we are inviting them to the conversation. They are at choice and only remain in the conversation as long as it feels collaborative.

These roles establish that the underlying intention of the process is for collaboration and mutual respect.

Chapter 7: Communication Framework

Conversation Initiator

The Conversation Initiator picks intention and mode cards and invites the Collaborator(s) to use the specific conversation mode to engage the topic of the Conversation Initiator's choosing.

Pitfalls

Being rude, inconsiderate, abrupt or overly directive may scare off collaborators and end the conversation before it starts.

Tips

Collaborators should feel invited to participate in the round. If you know about your conversation ahead of time, come prepared with any informing details or clear goals that may support the conversation.

Card Family:
Conversation Roles

http://healthy-relationships.us

Conversation Collaborator

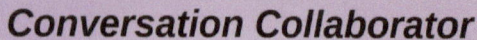

Conversation Collaborators are people who agree to play the round with the Conversation Initiator using the requested conversation mode. Once the round is complete, Collaborators can change roles and become a Conversation Initiator.

Pitfalls

Using other Conversation Modes in addition to or instead of the agreed Conversation Mode for the round.

Tips

Check in with yourself and your availability for the discussion before agreeing to the proposed intention and conversation mode.

Are you able to be collaborative?

Card Family:
Conversation Roles

http://healthy-relationships.us

Chapter 7: Communication Framework 79

Conversation Facilitator

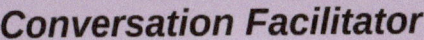

The Conversation Facilitator monitors the conversation. The Facilitator should be familiar with the various conversation modes and let the group know when it seems that a different mode is being used than agreed for the round.

Pitfalls

Interjecting or Interpreting for the Conversation Initiator and the Collaborator(s) unless that is asked for or approved first.

Tips

Review all the conversation mode cards before the game starts.

Pay close attention during the round and point out any Conversation Modes being used out of turn.

Card Family:
Conversation Roles

http://healthy-relationships.us

Conversation Goals / Intentions

Quite commonly, people will start having a conversation without even knowing what their intention is. Individuals may be speaking out from a place of reactivity in an effort to reduce their own stress or discomfort in the moment.

If we can get past this sense of urgency and more deeply understand the intentions of the conversation, we can then prepare ourselves to relate with the discussion in a way that feels more satisfying for all.

When we share our intentions with others, it opens up more opportunity for getting what we want.

We will now review the following Conversation Intentions. More specific intentions usually fall under one of the three main categories:

- Seed Planting
- Tending, Feeding, Nurturing
- Weeding and Clearing

The Conversation Initiator is responsible for stating their intention while making a Conversation Invitation and requesting a specific Communication Mode. You can read about Communication Modes and example invitations in the upcoming sections.

Seed Planting

In Seed Planting, we are bringing ideas to the table to see what takes root. These conversations can often be exploratory and end in agreements to take some action, gather more information or have a follow on conversation at another time.

Pitfalls

Be wary of Clearing / Weeding conversations disguised as Seed Planting.

Tips

Keep an open mind and take time consider other ideas that emerge. Consider reviewing Pro's and Cons of the situation.

Card Family:
Intentions

http://healthy-relationships.us

Tending, Feeding & Nurturing

Put your attention on a project or a person in a supportive way. This Conversation Mode could be used if you wanted to appreciate someone for work they are doing or tell them how much you enjoy their presence in your life. One could also use this card to inquire about the needs of others.

Pitfalls

Not being mindful of your own level of frustration or capacity for caregiving. Overextending yourself.

Tips

Tending, Feeding and Nurturing are best served with a loving heart.

Complete the round before you are feeling drained or tired.

**Card Family:
Intentions**

http://healthy-relationships.us

Weeding and Clearing

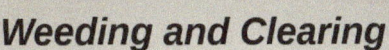

When ideas and life situations create tensions that come between us and disrupt the peace of the relationship, clearing conversations can help to create more connection, collaboration and friendliness to your interactions.

Pitfalls

Be wary of blaming Collaborators or blasting them with intensity.

Tips

Try speaking to collaborators with love, compassion and peace in your heart. Conversation Collaborators should use the Yellow and Red cards to moderate the speaker if the conversation gets heated.

**Card Family:
Intentions**

http://healthy-relationships.us

Navigating Tricky Conversations Skillfully

Communication Modes

Communication Modes describe our ways of sharing information and relating at the moment. Modes are described extensively in the Journey Kit chapter. Some examples are: Attentive Listening, Interpreting, Devil's Advocate, and Defensive.

You will see that modes are broken into a scale based on levels of assertiveness.
- Soft Modes
- Moderate Modes
- Assertive Modes
- Shadow Modes

You will also see Shadow Modes are included so that they may be identified when used UN-consciously or so that they may be requested for strengthening or purifying ideas and our presentation of the information.

Each of the modes, even the Shadow Modes, have a particular time and place where they may be requested by the Conversation Initiator.

Once you have reviewed each of the Communication Modes in the upcoming sections, you can familiarize yourself with how to know which mode to use in the Tips for Navigating Tricky Conversations Skillfully section.

Chapter 7: Communication Framework

Soft Modes

Soft Modes are well suited to use in situation of high intensity, distress or emotional charge. For example, people who are in a process of expressing their frustration are not interested in receiving advice. They are interested in having a chance to express themselves and vent their frustration. After that, they may then go into requesting advice while reverting into dismissing advice followed by more venting.

Soft Modes are excellent for giving a person who is expressing and exploring their own inner content an opportunity to feel seen, heard and supported in their experience.

From my coaching practice I can tell you that soft modes are the most powerful for DE-escalating intense emotional charge and getting to a place of integration.

Echoing can be such a powerful tool for creating Somatic Resonance that I'm surprised it is still legal!

Types of Soft Modes we will explore:

- Attentive Listening
- Echoing
- Reassurance

Navigating Tricky Conversations Skillfully

Attentive Listening

This round is all about the speaker experiencing being heard without interjection. Give your full attention to the speaker. Demonstrate understanding & empathy with body posture, eye contact, head nods, and "mm-hmms".

Pitfalls

Listeners often want to reply to the content of the speakers sharing with their own ideas, suggestions, objections, corrections.

Tips

Save any sharing, Interpretation, Echoing or other Conversation Modes for another round. Attentive Listeners may use the Yellow Speaker Moderation Cards if they notice their attention waning.

Card Family:
Soft Modes

http://healthy-relationships.us

Chapter 7: Communication Framework

Echoing

Repeat back to the speaker what you heard them say, using their own words, rather than paraphrasing or interpreting what they said. Try to add nothing to what the speaker said; just reflect back the speaker's own words.

Pitfalls

Using interpretation, advice, empathy, etcetera. These are all deviating from Echoing.

Tips

Just repeat the words only.

Start with, "I heard you say... I also heard..."

This may feel mechanical at first, yet can be very rewarding. It will feel more natural with practice.

Card Family:
Soft Modes

http://healthy-relationships.us

Reassurance

Reassurers inquire about expressed worries or fears, by first naming them: "Sounds like you're worried/scared about..."; second, asking for confirmation; and third, offering comfort: "I can understand how you'd feel...", or "I'd like to help however I can", or, "I imagine we can work that out."

Pitfalls

Being Dismissive of the speaker's concerns, being concise, simply Echoing the concern

Tips

Avoid trivializing speaker's fears or sounding condescending. Empathize with the speaker's situation. Only say what feels authentic & genuine.

Card Family:
Soft Modes

http://healthy-relationships.us

Chapter 7: Communication Framework 89

Moderate Modes

When volatility has waned and the situation still requires some delicate balance, we may want to use a Moderate Conversation Mode.

When using Moderate Modes, the conversation participants may engage the subject matter more deeply. There may also be more room for individuals to express varying viewpoints or question motives and goals (preferably without judgment).

When using Moderate Modes, conversation participants will want to maintain solidarity and respectful engagement of the discussion.

We will review the following Moderate Modes:

- Interpretation
- Empathy
- Check-in

Interpretation

Share the meanings you're making out of what the speaker says. Offer your ("morally neutral") interpretations of what you've heard. Some examples include: paraphrasing, making possible connections, suggesting deeper levels, and/or unnamed implications of what has been spoken.

Pitfalls

Including judgements (which carry the implication of "good" or "bad"), Including haphazard advice

Tips

Avoid smuggling such moral judgments of "right" or "wrong" into your responses. Try to *describe*, rather than *evaluate*, what is so.

Card Family:
Moderate Modes

http://healthy-relationships.us

Empathy
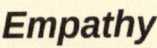

Empathizers hear about the emotional weather report, sensing the feelings and witnessing the person. Once the speaker has shared, an Empathizer may check-in with something like; "Wow, I really sense a deep level of (frustration) and hear how long you have been going through this. ..."

Pitfalls

Empathizer misrepresenting their emotional availability or shifting into other modes: Defensive, Advice etc.

Tips

Sink into "deep listening" where you hear the words and allow yourself to feel the emotions carried with the words. Be careful not to minimize the person's concerns or try to fix the problem.

Card Family:
Moderate Modes

http://healthy-relationships.us

Check-in

This is an investigative conversation where the Conversation Initiator requests some further information from the Collaborator(s) on a specific topic.

Pitfalls

Unfocused conversation, unregulated pacing, moving into other Conversation Modes, such as Interpreting or Advising, without proposing a new round

Tips

Keep Check-ins concise.

Notice when it's time to offer a Collaborator a chance to initiate a conversation with a new round.

Card Family:
Moderate Modes

http://healthy-relationships.us

Assertive Modes

Assertive Modes are best in times of lower emotional charge. When conversation participants are well resourced and interested in getting to the "heart of the matter".

Assertive modes are great for getting additional perspectives to help you figure out solutions to a problem or a situation.

Types of Assertive Modes:

- Advice
- Devil's Advocate
- Inspiration

Advice

Advice is about taking the best steps in moving forward. Ask clarifying questions about the situation, and more specifics about what kind of advice is wanted. Advice may include: mentioning additional considerations, next steps and other resources.

Pitfalls

Attachment to following the advice that is given. Judgments may also cloud advice.

Tips

Avoid making any judgments. It may also be ethical for Advisors to mention their background and biases, presenting their ideas so that the individual can make an informed choice.

Card Family:
Assertive Modes

http://healthy-relationships.us

Chapter 7: Communication Framework 95

Devil's Advocate

The Devil's Advocate explores the worst case scenarios. The intention is to give an opportunity to provide protection from failure or create back-up plans for problems that may arise. Devil's Advocate assumes that the idea has some merit/workability.

Pitfalls

Be cautious about ridiculing, shooting down or minimizing the idea at hand.

Tips

Be collaborative while sharing your ideas about what could fail/go wrong. Your sharing should be in support of ultimate success of the project/person

Card Family:
Assertive Modes

http://healthy-relationships.us

Inspiration

Sometimes we want to be feeling better or more motivated but we aren't there yet. A little inspiration can go a long way. Inspiration can range from: appreciating the person and acknowledging their existing accomplishments, all the way to facing the threat of what will happen through inaction.

Pitfalls

Using Devil's Advocate Mode: too many fear-based inspirations can cause further shut-down and overwhelm.

Tips

You may want to systematically progress through; repercussions of inaction, rewards for action, and new possibilities.

**Card Family:
Assertive Modes**

http://healthy-relationships.us

Chapter 7: Communication Framework

Shadow Modes

Shadow Modes often arise when we have requested some other Conversation Mode. Shadow Modes, by nature, are Communication Modes that usually work against our stated intention.

When observing the conversation in progress, you may notice that defensive or attacking conversationalists steal attention away from the original intention.

A less commonly observed occurrence of the dismissive mode is when people dismiss the appreciation of others, "oh it was nothing, I just..." (am going to minimize your appreciation.)

By understanding Shadow Modes we can acknowledge them in action and divert attention back to our original intention.

Conversationalists may also request someone use a Shadow Mode with them as a chance to practice and improve their own grounded presence while being met with Defensive or Attacking language.

Types of Shadow Modes we will explore:

- Dismissive
- Attacking
- Defensive

Navigating Tricky Conversations Skillfully

Defensive

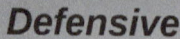

When one feels as though one's actions are being judged negatively one may begin to explain how they came to making those decisions or actions. Reactive Defenders may deflect by transition into Attacking.

Pitfalls

Getting distracted from the topic of the initial conversation, engaging in blaming or defending ideas

Tips

Point out Defensive language and behaviors when they emerge and consider reframing the conversation to make it more about one's relationship with the action and less about the other person (Defender).

Card Family:
Shadow Modes

http://healthy-relationships.us

Chapter 7: Communication Framework

Attacking

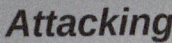

Attackers' actions do not elicit a sense of collaboration. An Attacker's intentions may be to: dis-credit, diminish or otherwise dominate the speaker. They may raise their voice, make assertive hand gestures, make hurtful or aggravating statements.

Pitfalls

Being Defensive, counter-attacking, withdrawing

Tips

Avoid answering attacking questions. Point out Attacking language and behaviors when they emerge. State, "I'm experiencing you as Attacking me. Would you be willing to share your ideas in a more friendly way?"

Card Family:
Shadow Modes

http://healthy-relationships.us

Dismissive

Dismissers diminish the speakers points by representing that what the speaker said is unworthy of consideration. They may ignore comments without responding or state that the speakers ideas are not important, without merit or relevance.

Pitfalls

Being defensive, allowing Dismissers to change the conversation topic, losing faith in one's own ideas

Tips

Point out Dismissive language and behaviors when they emerge. Represent self-confidence and bring the conversation back to discussing the points of interest.

Card Family:
Shadow Modes

http://healthy-relationships.us

Chapter 7: Communication Framework   101

Chapter 8

The Communication Cycle

In this chapter we will talk about the communication cycle using the card kit. Please keep in mind that the cards serve as a means to externalize the communication process and provide some grounding elements.

These approaches and the communication cycle can all be used even without the cards. Even if you don't plan on using the card kit, it's worth reading this chapter to understand how to use progressive communication cycles with recurring appreciation.

In this chapter we will explore:

- Consider your Intention
- Set Up the Cards if Available
- Establish Roles
- Establish Intentions
- Invite Collaborator(s) to a Round
- Using Moderation Cards and Tokens
- End with an Appreciation Round

Consider your Intention

Being clear on your underlying intention for the conversation makes all the difference in the trajectory and outcomes. Often times our intention for having conversation is to relieve our own stress. If we don't take time to consider our intentions then they start out ungrounded, and will often degrade into Shadow Modes.

By setting a productive or connective intention, you can then make a Conversation Invitation that feels inviting and friendly to others.

To keep it simple, we have given the basic framework of:

- Planting Seeds (introduce new ideas)
- Nurturing (take care of something already existing)
- Weeding & Clearing (resolve tension / conflict)

Make a Conversation Invitation

Conversation Invitations are important!

Taking the time to let someone know that you have an important topic that you want to discuss and that you want them in the conversation can be a really successful place to start from.

For example,

> "Judy, I would like to talk with you about the driveway parking situation. Are you available to talk with me about it on Tuesday or Thursday at 3pm?"

Once Judy responds with her availability you could then follow up with,

> "I would like to use the Communication Journey Kit to keep our conversation more fun and rewarding. Would that be OK with you?"

Chapter 8: The Communication Cycle 105

Reference the examples section for more Conversation Invitation examples.

Set Up the Cards if Available

Set up the cards so that you can see the titles of all the cards and they are grouped together by card families. Each card family has its own unique border color and card family icon in the lower right hand corner.

Lay the cards out in order of Roles, Intentions, Facilitation Cards, Soft Modes, Moderate Modes, Assertive Modes and Shadow Modes as pictured below.

Distribute an Equal amount of Appreciation Tokens to everyone in the conversation and set out the Clarifying Question Tokens for anyone to pick up during a round.

Establish Conversational Roles

Usually the person who has invited the other to the conversation would be the Conversation Initiator. The Conversation Initiator should pick up that role card for themselves, set it nearby, then hand the Conversation Collaborator card to the collaborator. When multiple collaborators are present, they may share the Conversation Collaborator Card. If there is a Conversation

Facilitator present they may take the Facilitator Card. If not, then the Conversation Initiator may also act as the facilitator for that round. Each round could have a new Conversation Initiator.

Establish Conversational Intentions

The Conversation Initiator will then select the appropriate intention card for the conversation they would like to propose. Once the Conversation Intention card is selected, the Conversation Initiator then begins the Communication Cycle by inviting the Conversation Collaborator(s) to a round.

Invite Collaborator(s) to a Round

Invite Conversation Collaborators to use a particular Communication Mode for the round. After the round is over, anyone can request a new round.

Using the Communication Cycle

1. Conversation Initiator invites the Conversation Collaborator(s) to a round using a specific Conversation Mode.

> "Judy, I would like to invite you to Collaborate with me in a Weeding and Clearing conversation about the parking situation. Would you be willing to offer me a round of Advice?"

- (optional) Users can read the [Advice] Mode card out loud before starting the round

If Judy agrees, then the Advice Mode card is placed next to the Weeding and Clearing Intention card.

2. The Conversation Initiator will then share more information with the Collaborator(s).

"When I come home at 6pm, all my housemates have already parked in the driveway and there are no spots on the street. I end up spending 45 minutes every night trying to find parking. I'm wondering if you have any ideas about how I can solve my frustrating parking problem and stop wasting my time."

3. The Collaborator uses the Specific Conversation Mode (Advice) requested by the Initiator.

Judy replies with,

"When I was living there, I used to carpool with Bill. Have you considered car pooling? Also, I believe the #47 bus goes directly past your work. Finally, maybe you could work out a car rotation agreement with your housemates or ask one of your house mates to move cars to street parking earlier in the day when it is available."

In some cases, the Conversation Collaborator may use a Conversation Mode other than the mode requested. In those cases, reference the examples section for Re-Orienting to the Conversation Mode or Re-Orienting to the Conversation Intention.

4. Finishing a Round: When the Conversation Initiator feels that the initial intention is satisfied for the round, the round is over.

"Those are some great ideas. I really appreciate you, Judy, for taking the time to hear me out and give me a few pointers about it."

　　Also, if a Collaborator or Facilitator plays the red card, the round is then over.

　　Once the round is over, the Initiator thanks the Collaborator(s) and Facilitator if present.

- (optional) The Conversation Initiator revisits the Mode card and asks the Collaborator if they are available to offer more of the requested mode.
- (optional) The Initiator asks the Collaborator if they would like to do another round or try a different mode.

5. Finishing with the conversation: All parties check in to see if they feel complete with the intentions established in step 1 and schedule more time to talk as needed.

"Is there anything else you would like to say or ask about it before we end the conversation?"

"No, I'm feeling complete for now, thank you!"

6. Completing the Conversation Journey: all parties share gratitude for the time, attention and anything else they would like to appreciate about the conversation or how each of the people in the conversation were supportive of the intention.

"Well Judy, I'd like to say that it feels really good to have someone to talk with about this. I really appreciate you for taking the time in your schedule to advise me about it. You gave me some valuable insight and I'm going to follow up on it."

Chapter 8: The Communication Cycle

Using Moderation Cards and Tokens
Each Communication Journey Kit comes with several types of Moderation cards.

The types of Moderation Cards are:

- Appreciation Tokens
- Clarifying Question Tokens
- Yellow Cards
- Red Card

Using Appreciation Tokens

The Appreciation Tokens should be distributed evenly between all participants at the beginning of the conversation. Tokens were created so that they can be given without interrupting during a round.

At any time, before, during or after a round, any participant may give an Appreciation Token to another participant in the round.

Some participants may be grateful for having the person join them in the round and start the round by giving out appreciation in the very beginning.

Also, if a participant says something particularly useful, vulnerable or nice, we may want to show them that we appreciate how they are showing up and encourage this behavior by placing the token near the other participant.

Appreciation tokens are a great way to celebrate the fun of the game and keep it feeling like a rewarding process for everyone.

Using Clarifying Question Tokens

There are multiple Clarifying Question Tokens per kit. Tokens were created so that they can be shared without interrupting the speaker during a round. These tokens should be placed nearby for Collaborators to pick up during the round.

If a Collaborator has questions, they can pick up the token and set it aside to indicate a question on the current subject. The speaker may continue to talk without changing course of the discussion. The speaker may also take a cue from seeing the Clarifying Question token and fill in the missing details.

If the question is answered before the end of the round, the Conversation Collaborator may return the token to its original position.

Depending on the intention of the round and the Communication Mode being selected, the Speaker may or may not offer to answer the questions of the Collaborator.

For example, in the case of Advice, when the Speaker finishes the initial sharing, they may say:

> "I see that you have 3 Clarifying Question Tokens there, would you like to ask me some clarifying questions about what I just shared?"

In the case of an Attentive Listening or Echoing round, the conversation Initiator might respond with:

> "I see that you have some Clarifying Question Tokens there. Would you be willing to Echo what you heard so far?"

Once the Echoing is complete the Speaker could respond with:

> "Thank you so much for Echoing me, I really feel seen and heard by you. Would you like to propose a new round with the Check-in Mode and ask me your Clarifying Questions?"

Using Yellow and Red Moderation Cards

When sharing important topics, speakers can often become passionate and animated. Also, if the conversation has been repressed for some time, then it's likely that there might be a lot to say once the conversation gets rolling.

Saying a lot in the conversation or speaking passionately can be OK, so long as everyone in the conversation is well resourced for it and feeling respected.

However, when that passion turns into a tidal wave of passionate loud talking or unchecked frustrations, listeners in the conversation can become overwhelmed or withdraw as they feel the respect diminish.

The Yellow and Red Moderation Cards give Collaborators a chance to alert the speaker that they are losing the attention of the Collaborator.

The Yellow Card basically alerts the speaker to slow down, take a breath and check in with how they are delivering the information. There are two Yellow Cards provided with the Communication Journey Kit.

The Red Card alerts the speaker that the Collaborator is now "Full" and that their attention or interest for the round has expired. Once the Red Card has been presented, the round is over and the speaker should thank the Collaborator(s) and give appreciation for the round. The Collaborator(s) may also express some appreciation as well, so long as it's authentic.

> "That was clearly some important stuff! I really hear you! I'm glad you got a chance to share all of that and maybe we can come back to it when things settle down a bit."

Chapter 8: The Communication Cycle   113

Moderation: Yellow Card

The speaker may be speaking too fast or too assertively. Please try taking a few breaths and slowing down the conversation. If the Speaker does slow down the Collaborator may leave the Yellow card in Play or return it to the deck. If two Yellow Cards are currently "In Play", the next card played may be the Red Card.

Pitfalls

Speakers may be irritated by the Yellow card and speak even more assertively.

Tips

Be mindful that this is a connection game and the idea is to keep everyone in the conversation.

http://healthy-relationships.us

Moderation: Red Card

Thank you, the round is Over!

The Collaborator(s) may put the Red Card "into play" at any time. The Red Card is best served after two Yellow Cards are already "In Play".

Pitfalls

Game players can be enticed to continue the conversation after the red card is shown. Please avoid temptation and respect the end of the round.

Tips

Every person playing game share something they appreciate from the round to help bring a sense of completion

http://healthy-relationships.us

End with Appreciation and Satisfaction

In team sports, we often remember those final parting shots right at the end of the game. When people talk about a basketball game and mention who won, they will often discuss that last 3-point shot that either made it in or did not make it in. What about the other 76 points scored in the game up to those final moments? All those moments leading up to the end are often overshadowed by the final moment. This is also true with our conversations. How we end a conversation can often have a greater impact than most of the conversation itself.

After each Communication Cycle has finished and before the conversation is over, share a round of appreciation. Reference the examples section for sample appreciations.

The more appreciation you bring to each conversation, the more satisfaction you will have in your own life.

There is a very real body response that happens when sharing appreciation. Effectively, we are saying "Yes" to something about the moment and this invokes the sensations of Somatic Resonance. This is a continuous positive feedback loop. The more time we spend in appreciating and saying yes to the moment, the more our posture changes from hard and rejecting to open and allowing.

When human beings allow themselves to be open to the flow of energy, the sensations of energy flowing are often felt as pleasure. When there is a posture of rejection and static tensegrity, this creates a dynamic where we consume our energy to resist something in existence. While there can be some benefit to resisting undesirable outcomes, it comes at an energetic cost.

In being mindful of these dynamics, we always have the option to uplift ourselves and others by overtly mentioning what it is we are appreciating about the moment, our situation or the actions of others.

Additionally, overtly mentioning our appreciation is also likely to reinforce desirable behavior and support us in getting more of what we want. Even if the same situation never happens again, the act of appreciating a moment gives us a second opportunity to be nourished by the original incident. The more we can remember that something was satisfying, the more satisfaction we will get from that one moment.

Finally, ending with appreciation will also foster a sense of deeper trust with others in the conversation. When you end with appreciation, the other participants will depart feeling respected, honored, and valued. This will lead to easier conversations in the future as you inspire and facilitate more trust.

> "I know that this conversation was potentially stressful and that I got tense at times. I wanted to take a moment to appreciate you for being committed to working it out with me and taking the time to talk about it.
>
> Now that we've talked, I'm feeling more easeful, friendlier and more relaxed. Thank you so much for talking with me with love and respect. I really am grateful to you for making it safe for us to have conversations like this."

Chapter 8: The Communication Cycle

Part 3: Improving Your Conversational Competence

Chapter 9

Tips for Navigating Tricky Topics

First of all, let me just say that...

> "there is always room for more Grace."

So my first tip is to be compassionate with yourself and others.

If you are really serious about getting good results, share this book and discuss it with others. Talk about these communication modes and see what others think. Try it out in conversation and see what kind of results you get.

Take time to do the self-study activities in this book and apply the concepts to conversations you are already having.

In this chapter, we will discuss:

- Should there be a Conversation Facilitator?
- Providing Support, One at a Time!
- Hearing the Story, One at a Time!
- Learn to Identify Communication Modes

Should There Be a Facilitator?
How do you know when it's time to invite a third party to the conversation?

When there is emotional volatility or vulnerability for one or more of the conversation participants, you may want to invite a Conversation Facilitator.

Often times couples are resistant to bringing in a Conversation Facilitator because they think it means that their relationship is broken or that they cannot handle it on their own. While either of these statements might be true, it is also true that your relationship or the situation you are discussing might be worth having it be well supported for mutual benefit.

When you add a Conversation Facilitator, you bring in more Conversational Resources to support your goal. This shows that you value the people and the situation enough to invest in the outcome.

It is worth mentioning that some couples or individuals may have fears of being judged or treated unfairly by a facilitator. It is important to understand the needs and concerns of all involved and choose a facilitator who supports each person in feeling valued and respected.

Providing and Requesting Support, One at a Time!
Often times couples will get into a situation where both of them need support and are ready for it to be their turn to be heard, seen, supported, and to be right!

While it's true that both of them can be right at the same time, even with conflicting view-points, if two people show up needing support and nobody else is there, it can create an under-resourced conversation.

What does this mean? Even if you both really want to talk, it may not be the best climate and timing to have the conversation and get the outcomes that you want. If you need support, be sure to ask for it from someone who seems well-resourced to support you. If you are offering support, make sure you are well-resourced to offer the support that's being requested.

If two people really do need support today and nobody else is available then it can be a wise approach to schedule two separate talks with a 30-minute break in between.

Do not agree to support someone in conversation if you are not ready and available to do so. If you find yourself under-resourced in the conversation, request changes in the Conversation Pacing or request to end the conversation sooner.

It is extremely important to make only genuine offers. If you aren't ready, then consider deferring to a later time. You could say something like:

> "I can tell this is a really important topic and I really want to discuss it with you. At the moment I know I'm a little distracted and need to take care of some other things.
>
> Could we have a special time to talk about it when I could be really present to hear your concerns? Perhaps tonight after dinner might work well for both of us. Thank you for inviting me to this conversation and I'm looking forward to talking with you about it."

Hearing One Story at a Time

Heated conversations can go from bad to worse when communicators are trying to argue for whose version of the truth is correct. Communicators may feel urgency to correct the story of another when it conflicts their own version of what "actually happened."

Often in volatile conversations, the actual technical details of what is being said aren't really that important. An emotional speaker will often desire to be echoed or receive empathy. Once a volatile speaker is echoed and presented with empathy, the emotional pressure will often diffuse. This diffusion gives rise to the possibility for a new conversation that may allow for the discussion of some of the deeper details of what has been said.

If a responder does not agree with the details presented, they can simply say, "I heard you say..." and " I also heard you say ...". This gives the responder a chance to acknowledge what's being said so that diffusion may occur, without the responder actually discussing or agreeing with the content of what's been said. Reference the Echoing mode for more information.

Learn to Identify Modes Being Used by Others

Even if you are clear about what Conversation Mode you would like to request or have requested, that does not guarantee that your collaborator will actually only use the requested mode. Also, in life, we have conversations with people who aren't always intending to collaborate.

By practicing observing conversations and naming which mode is being used, you will also be able to go deeper and discern the intentions of the people in the conversation. It can be very rewarding to watch the conversations of others without having investment in the conversation to build your mastery of identifying modes. You can do this while watching movies or at work or on the phone.

You don't have to name the Communication Modes out loud, just practice identifying the mode for yourself. If you have someone in your life who has also read this book or used the Communication Journey Kit, then you can make conversations more fun by naming Communication Modes together.

Chapter 9: Tips for Navigating Tricky Topics

Pay close attention to the Shadow Modes. Study the dynamics and intentions of conversationalists who use Shadow Modes. Learn compassionate ways to interact with people who are using Shadow Modes and negotiate healthful conversation. Sometimes the healthiest Conversation Mode is Silence. We have not yet added the Silence Mode card to the Communication Journey Kit, but feel free to request it when it seems as though collaboration has deteriorated or when some integration and consideration time is warranted.

126 Navigating Tricky Conversations Skillfully

Chapter 10

Facilitating

As a Conversation Facilitator, you have the power to shepherd the conversation towards the most rewarding conversation for all involved. Having a third person in the conversation who has the authority to give guidance and feedback during a tricky conversation can be extremely helpful.

In the following segments we will outline some helpful tips for keeping the conversation feeling rewarding for all.

In this chapter, we will discuss:

- The Myth of Understanding
- Monitoring Conversational Resources
- Navigating Climates
- Conversation Pacing
- Verbally Naming Modes in Use
- Conversational Coherence

The Myth of Understanding

People often think that if they were understood, then it would fix everything. There is often an assumption that if the other people understood them then they might act differently or that the situation would not occur. The reality of the matter is that this mentality creates a trap that leaves everyone in the conversation feeling exhausted. Most Tricky Conversations are created by individuals reacting unconsciously to their own discomfort or some type of Cognitive Dissonance without understanding their own inner tensions.

What this means is that, if there is emotional content involved, the conversation may need to be longer than it would take to simply convey the technical information about it. If it were just technical data, the content could be clearly stated one time and then the discussion would be complete. However, for a conversation with emotional content, an emotionally charged participant may need to repeat themselves several / many times to feel like they fully expressed the point. It is important to understand if the intention of the conversation is to reduce stress. If this is identified, then a Nurturing or Clearing Mode may be selected and the conversation can be well resourced for emotional support.

If it is not clear that it's a stress reduction conversation, then the listener may become frustrated when the speaker repeats themselves several times and rejects advice etc.

Monitoring Conversation Resources

If you are taking on the role of Conversation Facilitator, you will want to be tracking the Conversational Resources. If you see that these resources are depleted, then it may be time to add some appreciation, propose ending the round, redirect to the initial intention, take a break or schedule another discussion at a later time.

Some Conversational Resources include:

- Time: Is there enough for the conversation?
- Privacy: Will there be any interruptions?
- Emotional Stability: Are participants combative?
- Attention / Cognitive Availability / Interest: Can participants continue to focus on the topic at hand?

Navigating Climates

When Facilitating a conversation, it is important to be aware of the emotional climate of each of the participants. If the conversation participants have had a long / stressful day, a recent loss, or increasing responsibilities, the climate may be Tense before the conversation even starts.

There is often some existing conversation or circumstance that the current situation emerges from. That situation may be creating tension within an individual or between individuals.

You may notice conversation participants experiencing being

- Relaxed
- Tense
- Highly Reactive

You may also observe yourself or other participants engaging in potentially destructive conversation approaches. We generally refer to potentially destructive Communication Modes as "Shadow Modes".

Watch for use of any Shadow Modes. If you see a Shadow Mode being used, you can name it and request more collaboration.

> "It seems like maybe you are using the [Defensive] Mode. Would you be willing to return to the agreed upon [Echoing] Mode for this round? If you like, we could then follow with another round to address those other points you mentioned."

Navigating Tricky Conversations Skillfully

Facilitators may optionally point out or even read aloud the [Defensive] and [Echoing] Mode cards before re-convening the round.

If you notice that the conversation is more emotionally pregnant, try using Soft Modes first to slow down the conversation and encourage conversation that creates Somatic Resonance. Somatic Resonance techniques are described previously in this book.

You can further dismantle destructive conversation by advocating for "Clean Communication." Review the following section on Right Mindfulness for Observances, Abstinations and Liberating Language. As the Conversation Facilitator, you are invited to assertively name Shadow Modes when they emerge and re-orient the conversation to the mutually rewarding and respectful intentions.

Pacing

While individuals may be able to receive common information quickly and easily, new concepts or emotionally pregnant topics require more time to integrate fully. Depending on the amount of volatility, you can select either a Soft, Moderate or Assertive mode. Assertive Modes are only recommended for when emotional reactivity is low.

If there is a lot of emotional reactivity or emotional integration, start with Soft Modes, especially the Echoing mode.

Repeating the same information several times may feel strange, yet allows for much deeper integration than just saying it one time. Repeating information by using the Echoing Mode can be a very effective means of slowing down the pace of the conversation and getting more rich rewards with the topic at hand.

Remember, for emotional conversations, it's not about understanding the specific information at hand, it's about having time to sit with the discomfort and "unpack it" enough so that diffusion and integration can be achieved.

While repetition, Echoing and Interpretation may seem like slow going, using these modes at the appropriate time actually facilitate

Chapter 10: Facilitating 131

things moving faster than using any other mode. These approaches allow the speaker to get to the heart of the matter in a way that allows for emotional unpacking. This unpacking paves the way for new realities and perspectives to emerge.

Verbally Naming Modes in Use

Depending on their goals and emotional climate, conversationalists engage in a wide range of Communication Modes. Being able to name modes at play can help you to reorient the conversation into accomplishing your goals.

In one example, a friend had given me an expensive gift. When I thanked him for his generosity, he kept the conversation very short and dismissed my appreciation stating that it was "no big deal because..."

I came away from the conversation feeling unsettled. After consideration, I brought it up with them again later. I said:

> "In our conversation the other day, I left feeling somewhat unfinished with the conversation. I had tried to appreciate you, but then you dismissed my appreciation. I was hoping we could talk about it some more."

The person replied that he had noticed it as well, and that he was glad that I brought it up. He went on to reveal about his own social training and how "Southern Hospitality" often includes providing a great deal and representing the actions as inconsequential or simple to provide. We had a deeper conversation about it and we both acknowledged that it was a significant gift that felt good to both give and receive.

You can find more examples of naming Communication Modes at play in the examples section.

Conversational Coherence

In its simplest version, Coherence means to stick together.

In more eloquent interpretations we find that coherence can also be observed as many parts working together harmoniously.

For Conversational Coherence to exist, the conversation discussion must stay close enough to the intention of the discussion and remain in manageable enough sizes not to exceed or underwhelm the conversation participants.

As you may have guessed already, Climate and Pacing can hugely impact Conversational Coherence. For example, if one participant starts blaming another, then the collaboration deteriorates and Coherence is lost.

Watch for the level of attention and engagement of conversation participants. If it seems like participants' focus of attention is elsewhere, consider reorienting the conversation or ending the round.

To learn more ideas about reestablishing Conversational Coherence, visit the sections on conversational tension, pacing and repairing blowout in chapter 4.

Chapter 10: Facilitating 133

Chapter 11

Examples

This chapter contains basic examples that you may adapt to your own situations. While you could repeat much of what has been written here word for word and have it be effective, it is intended to be a guide for you to create your own meaningful, heartfelt responses.

It is also worth mentioning that you should only say what feels authentic. Some people may think it's "out of reach" to be appreciative and friendly in the face of a difficult or stressful topic. However if you can maintain a sense of gratitude and respect for the person contributing their time and attention to the conversation, then you are bound to get more effective results.

In this chapter I will introduce:

- Opening with Appreciation and Intention Setting
- Creating Conversation Invitations
- Verbally Naming Modes in Use
- Reorient to the Conversation Intention
- Reorient to the requested Conversation Mode
- Requesting a Pause in the Conversation
- Close with Appreciations

Opening with Appreciation Intention Setting

Your opening statements set the tone of the conversation to come. Starting out with appreciation can put conversation participants at ease in the beginning and create a rich environment for collaboration.

> "Thank you so much for taking the time to talk with me. It's really important to me that we can be respectful and collaborative with each other and it means a lot to me that you would make the time to be in the conversation."

Optional:

{Unsolicited Safe-porting / Reassurance}

> "I also know that this has been a stressful topic in the past and I want you to know that I'm interested in this being an easy conversation for us both and that I'm interested in you getting your needs met here also."

Creating Conversation Invitations

Individuals often have resistance to tricky conversations because they may want to avoid stress or fear of loss. Crafting conversation invitations that address the invited party's needs can help create more interest and collaboration.

> "… I know that there has been some tension about the Friday night driveway parking and I would love to have a friendly conversation together about it at some time that works well for you. Would you be willing to discuss it with me on Tuesday at 6pm

or is there some other time that might work better for you?"

Optional:

{ Safe-porting Yourself }

" I appreciate that you are ready to talk about it Right Now, and also I think we might be able to have a more relaxed conversation about it if I have a few days to get my thoughts together about it."

Verbally Naming Modes in Use

Being able to track and name which Communication Modes are being used in the moment can help to raise awareness with conversation participants and build a bridge toward asking for the Communication Mode you would like to receive.

"Thank you for being in the conversation with me. I appreciate your time and attention on this.

It sounds like at the moment you are …

… Echoing what I had to say"

… offering some Reassurance"

… Interpreting what I said and giving some deeper insights"

… wanting to Check-in with me about some aspects of what I said"

… playing Devil's Advocate"

… offering some Advice"

… shifting the conversation to be about you" (Defensive)

… in disagreement about what I have said" (Attacking)

… invalidating what I was sharing" (Dismissive, Invalidation)

… expressing some of your own frustrations about it" (Venting)

Reorient to the Conversation Intention

When conversations become emotionally unstable, mired in minutiae, or otherwise off track, being able to reorient to the initial conversation intention can be an essential skill.

"… I think what we are discussing here has value, and I also notice we are getting a little off track from the initial Intention of this conversation.

Our original Intention was to maintain a friendly disposition while gathering information about the Friday night driveway usage.

I'd be open to scheduling some time to talk more about the street parking, but for now can we get back to the friendly Friday night driveway parking discussion?"

Reorient to the requested Conversation Mode

Conversations can easily get off track and also not every person is highly skilled in understanding what kind of engagement the conversation initiator wants or how to effectively do that. The Communication Modes listed in this book take practice.

It's quite likely that even when someone is trying to echo, they may interpret or accidentally slide into advising. It is helpful to be able to acknowledge what's happening at the moment and lovingly request the kind of support / engagement you would like.

> "... I appreciate your insights and your attention. I think what's going to be most helpful for me right now is if you were willing to respond with some (Reassurance, Echoing, Empathy, Interpretation etc.)
>
> Would you be willing to try (Echoing) what I have just said?
>
> Would you be willing to give me some (Reassurance) about it?
>
> I think I might feel most deeply seen and understood by you if you were willing to give me some (Empathy) about what I just shared."

Optional:
Safe-port the responder by stating a willingness to try the other mode after the one you requested.

Navigating Tricky Conversations Skillfully

{ Redirect to Echoing With Safe-porting }

"I know you have some (questions, disagreement) about what I said and I'm willing to talk about it further, but can we first confirm what you heard me say? Would you be willing to please just say the words that you heard me say?"

Requesting a Pause in the Conversation

When conversations are moving quickly and emotional volatility is high, taking breaks in the conversation can help everyone involved to feel more at ease and respected. Also there may be some information expressed that a conversation participant wants to consider more before moving ahead in the discussion.

Short Conversational Pause

"Wow, I notice I'm feeling a lot of stress right now. My heart rate is elevated, my face feels hot, my jaw is clenched and my stomach is all knotted up! Can we take a pause in the conversation for just a moment? I'd like to feel a little more relaxed before we proceed."

NOTICE: I did not recommend pointing out the emotions of others. For example, it may be inflammatory or destructive to project "it seems like you are really (angry, frustrated) right now and we should talk about it later."

Making a statement like this is bound to make the situation worse by blaming the other person and putting them on the defensive. Also it gives them a chance to refute your assertion and keep the conversation in conflict.

By clearly stating what you are experiencing for yourself in terms of bodily sensations, you are able to stay out of the story making and share information that is irrefutable by the responder. This provides an excellent foothold to make a request from.

Requesting a Follow Up Conversation
> " I appreciate that you are ready to talk about it Right Now, and also I think we might be able to have a more relaxed conversation about it if I have a few days to get my thoughts together about it. Would Tuesday at 6pm work for you or is there some other time that works better?"

Closure with Appreciation
What happens at the end of an interaction is what individuals will often remember most... how did it end? Ending the conversation with appreciation has both the person hearing and the person saying the appreciation feeling more satisfied by the conversation. This closing appreciation will serve well to create trust and rapport in approaching other topics in future conversations.

> "Thank you so much for being in this conversation with me...
>
> I know at some points it was stressful for me and I appreciate you for being committed to working it out with me. I also want to thank you for helping make it easy to talk about. I feel blessed to have an honorable friend like you and to be treated with such respect... I'm glad we can talk through things and work it out together. Thank you!"

Optionally:
> "I also want to appreciate you for when you said,

"..." It really clicked for me and I got a sense of what's going on. I didn't realize how much you were being impacted by this and I'm glad we were able to talk about it."

Chapter 11: Examples

Chapter 12

Self-Study

The Self-Study chapter will guide you in mastering your skills in Connective Communication. Each exercise is designed to build your skill so that when you are in your own conversations later, you can naturally and effectively use the skills when needed.

Completing the Self-Study is an essential part of this book. I recommend every person who read the book actually complete the exercises. Don't just read the book and believe me. There is no substitute for experience. Spend time investigating, do the research and develop your own skills. This book is just a starting point, it's up to you to be able to integrate the material and master it enough to know how and remember to skillfully apply it in tricky conversations.

Immersion students have access to completing the self-study exercises online. See the section on Personal Immersion Training for more information.

- Self-Study: Collect all the Communication Modes
- Self-Study: Use all four Yogic Keys
- Self-Study: Observe Emotional Climates

Self-Study: Collect all the Communication Modes

Mastering the Communication Modes is an essential part of this communication framework. One way to build mastery in modes is to assertively pay attention to what mode people are using when you listen to conversation. This can be done while listening to conversations in a movie, on the telephone or in person.

We like to make it more fun by calling it a Conversation Mode Scavenger Hunt!

On a sheet of paper, write down the names of each of the modes and then write down where and when you found the mode. You can also make notes of anything else you observed about the climate and how well the mode seemed to work at the moment.

Soft Modes:
- Attentive Listening
- Echoing
- Reassurance

Moderate Modes:
- Interpretation
- Empathy
- Check-in

Assertive Modes
- Advice
- Devil's Advocate
- Inspiration

Shadow Modes:
- Attacking
- Defensive
- Dismissive

Immersion Program Students can access the Conversation Mode Scavenger Hunt and their Conversation Logs online.

Chapter 12: Self Study

Self-Study: Use all 4 Yogic Keys

Each of the Yogic Keys has its own right time and place. Make sure you are using the right keys with the right people at the right time. For the sake of self-study, you could even try intentionally using a mismatched key and see what kind of results you get.

Review the section on the Four Yogic Keys and then create your own worksheet. Write down each of the four keys, when you used them and what the results were.

Personal Immersion students can access the Four Yogic Keys worksheet and Conversation Logs online.

The Four Yogic Keys:

- Compassion for Suffering People
- Friendliness for Happy People
- Delight in Virtuous Behavior
- Disregard / Equanimity with Non-Virtuous Behavior

Self Study: Observe Emotional Climates

Regardless of what climate would be convenient for us in any moment, the fact is that every person has a range of emotional states and at any given moment, we could find them somewhere in between their highest high and lowest low.

True conversation masters can gauge the climate of the moment and approach the conversation appropriately.

To study emotional climates, make a worksheet that includes the three emotional climates and log three conversations for each climate.

Climates:

- Relaxed
- Tense
- Highly Reactive

For each conversation write down any contributing factors for the climate, what Communication Modes were used and what was the outcome. Reference the following example.

Highly Reactive:

Title: volatile conversation after 10-hour car drive with three kids.

Contributing factors: see title... also we did not eat all day and were very irritable.

Description: got in a heated debate about parking and used both Attacking and Defensive Modes, finished with blaming.

Outcomes: both adults parted angry and frustrated.

Insights: when conversational resources are low, compassion and silence can both be golden.

Personal Immersion students may access the Emotional Climates worksheet and Conversation Logs online.

Chapter 12: Self Study   **149**

150   Navigating Tricky Conversations Skillfully

Chapter 13

Next Steps

If you would like to take your Connective Communication skills to the next level, you can take the following next steps:

- Complete the Self-Study Chapter Exercises
- Watch Connective Communication Videos Online
- Join the Connective Communication Newsletter
- Order the Communication Journey Kit
- Give this Book as a Gift
- Request Facilitation
- Request a Group Presentation
- Take the Personal Immersion Training
- Become a Connective Communication Coach
- Submit Feedback

Complete the Self-Study Chapter Exercises

I said it before and I will say it again. Reading this book is not a substitute for personal experience. Understanding the materials is only the beginning of creating your own healthy conversation habits.

The Self-Study chapter will guide you in mastering your skills in Connective Communication. Each exercise is designed to build your skill so that when you are in your own conversations later, you can naturally use the skills when needed.

Completing the Self-Study is an essential part of this book and I recommend every person who read the book actually complete the exercises. Don't just read the book and believe me, spend time investigating, do the research and develop your own skills. This book is just a starting point, it's up to you to be able to integrate the material and master it enough to apply it in conversation effectively when needed.

Immersion students have access to completing the self-study exercises online. See the section on Personal Immersion Training for more information.

Watch Videos Online

You can view our videos on the Healthy Relationships website at:

http://healthy-relationships.us

Join the Connective Communication Newsletter

You can join our newsletter online at the Healthy Relationships website at:

http://healthy-relationships.us

Chapter 13: Next Steps 153

Get the Communication Journey Kit
The Communication Journey Kit can be essential to introducing the Communication Modes to others in order to get the kind of conversation you want. Having something printed out can give much more validity to the framework of the conversation than words by themselves. When people can see what you have in mind, the situation becomes less mysterious and you may have more success in enrolling the type of conversation you want.

The Communication Journey Kit also helps groups to create a shared language in communication styles that may allow the group to more easily deal with emotionally volatile situations and Shadow Modes as they appear.

You can order the Communication Journey Kit online at the Healthy Relationships website at http://healthy-relationships.us

Give this Book as a Gift
If you purchase "Navigating Tricky Conversations Skillfully" online, you may optionally specify to purchase as it a gift. Place your order at the Healthy Relationships website:

http://healthy-relationships.us

The name and address you provide as the billing address will appear on the packing slip so the recipient knows you sent the gift. If your gift order includes items intended for different recipients, make sure you enter a gift message for each item.

You may also purchase this book in electronic version for Kindle.

Request Facilitation

Facilitation is available both remotely via teleconference or Skype and also in person.

If you have a special need challenge, we can travel to you and provide support for individuals, families and businesses.

If you would like to schedule facilitation, please use our online request form at http://healthy-relationships.us/contact

Request a Group Presentation

As of the writing of this book, the author has presented many custom-tailored workshops including:

- Applying Body Wisdom in Conversation
- Fundamentals of Yogic Interpersonal Relating
- Navigating Tricky Conversations Skillfully
- Turning Bad Conversations into Satisfying Conversations
- Conversation Mode Practice Groups
- Getting more Yes

We can also offer more specific workshops for your group needs.

If you would like a group presentation, please use our online request form at http://healthy-relationships.us/contact

Excel in Connective Communication

Would you like to share Connective Communication with others?

We offer both Personal Immersion Training and Connective Communication Facilitator Training.

Positions are also available for Connective Communication Educators.

Personal Immersion Training

Personal Immersion Training can be done online via the online training videos, forum, online journaling assignments and one-on-one video or in-person training sessions.

Personal Immersion will give you the practice you need to:

- Interpret Body Wisdom
- Skillfully Identify Communication Modes Being Used
- Identify Hidden Agendas
- Create Satisfying Responses with Liberating Language
- Craft Questions That Solicit The Type of Engagement You Desire

Connective Communication Coaches Training

Connective Communication Coaches Training builds on the immersion training. Facilitators will first complete the Personal Immersion Training before completing the Facilitator Training and Testing.

Facilitators demonstrate core competencies in:

- Creating Conversational Coherence
- Deescalating Emotional Volatility
- Conflict Resolution
- Building Team Rapport and Collaborative Spirit

Facilitators must demonstrate mastery of the core competencies in order to receive endorsement and permission to use the Connective Communication Coach title. Endorsed coaches may also join the Connective Communication Education core team.

Submitting Feedback

I intend to improve and expand this resource in a second edition. If you have any suggestions for additions and edits, please email yogi@ramadin.com with "NTCS Feedback" in your subject line.

Chapter 13: Next Steps

Thanks again for reading this book. May it inspire and support you in co-creating mutually satisfying relationships for many years to come.

May you be deeply nourished by the blessings in your life.

Peace be with you, all ways.

_/|_

Warmly,

Yogi Ramadin

Bibliography

J. Thomas Russell & W. Ronald Lane (2002) Kleppner's Advertising Procedure. Upper Saddle River, N.J: Prentice Hall.

Franklin, B. (1744). Poor Richard's Almanack, Printed and sold by B. Franklin

Festinger, L. (1957) A Theory of Cognitive Dissonance. Stanford, CA: Stanford University Press.

Cherry K. (n.d.). What Is Cognitive Dissonance?. About.com. Retrieved from http://psychology.about.com/od/cognitivepsychology/f/dissonance.htm

Yuna (2013). Gold [Recorded by Adventure Club]. On Calling All Heroes [CD]. Location: BMG Rights Management LLC

Sri Swami Satchidananda (2008) The Yoga Sutras of Patanjali. Buckingham, Virginia: Integral Yoga Publications.

Alphabetical Index

Allurement..33, **36,** 37
Appreciation...16, 28, 33, **34,** 43, 44, 45, 54, 67, 97, 103, 105, 109, 110, 115, 131, 135, 136, 141
Appreciation Tokens..16, **109**
Blowout, repairing..**45**
Cognitive Dissonance......................47, **48,** 49, 51, 52, 58, 59, 128
Cognitive Integration...**53, 58**
Collaboration...........24, 29, 33, **36,** 39, 45, 60, 76, 125, 129, 132, 136
Communication Cycle...45, 103, **106,** 115
Communication Modes....16, 18, 29, 45, 75, 84, 97, 124, 129, 131, 145, 146, 148, 153
    Assertive Modes...............................66, 84, **93,** 105, 130, 146
    Moderate Modes...30, 84, **89,** 105, 146
    Shadow Modes........18, 29, 30, 45, 64, 66, 84, **97,** 104, 105, 125, 129, 130, 146, 153
    Shadow Modes..29
    Soft Modes.................30, 66, 84, **85,** 105, 130, 146
Conversation Invitations....................33, **38,** 39, 104, 135, 136
Conversation Pacing..**43,** 123, 127
Conversation Resources........................27, **28,** 45, 128
Conversation Roles...75, 76
Conversational Climate...**27,** 29
Conversational Tension..5, 43, **44**
Diffusion.....................30, 47, 48, 53, **54,** 55, 56, 124, 130
Emotional Climate..........................27, **28,** 65, 131, 145, 148
Emotional Climate, Facilitation......................................129
Emotional Climate, Navigating.......................................**30**
Goals, Stated..**24**
Goals, Unstated...**25**
Liberating Language...............59, 63, 67, **68,** 69, 130, 155
Safe-porting..25, 33, **37,** 136, 137, 140
Somatic Resonance....34, 38, 47, 48, **49,** 50, 51, 52, 60, 67, 68, 85, 115, 130
Terminal language..52, **67,** 68
Transference..47, **52,** 53
Yamas and Niyamas...................................63, **64,** 65, 68

Index

www.ingramcontent.com/pod-product-compliance
Lightning Source LLC
Chambersburg PA
CBHW041619220426
43661CB00046B/1508